Advance Praise for *Always a Guest*

"Barbara Brown Taylor unleashes biblical wisdom like no other preacher I've ever heard or read. She meets us so hospitably in our messy humanity, and she reminds us of divine grace in her own beautiful, powerful way. Texts I've heard a thousand times feel new again. Ancient stories take on modern meaning. Love leaps off the page. And I feel God's tender embrace as if for the first time."

—Jeff Chu, author, *Does Jesus Really Love Me?*,
and cocurator, Evolving Faith

"I am incapable of being chill about this book or anything Barbara Brown Taylor writes, so brace yourself. She is one of my favorite writers, and this collection of her sermons will show you why she is also one of our generation's greatest preachers. On themes from anxiety to beauty, resurrection to doubt, wisdom, and telling the truth, Taylor does what all great preachers do: she proclaims the gospel. Each sermon is a wide and good feast that will feed us for years to come."

—Sarah Bessey, author, *Miracles and Other Reasonable Things*
and *Jesus Feminist*

"I first met Barbara Brown Taylor's breathtaking prose in *Leaving Church: A Memoir of Faith*. I read it when I desperately needed to remember that I was '. . . still held in arms I could not see.' Since then, I've had the honor to share sacred space with Barbara, spaces in which we are both sharing words from our heads and hearts. When I hear her speak, I'm mesmerized at the stunning tonic of intellect, breathtaking prose, rigorous research, and humble humor with which she offers wisdom and insight.

"To read Barbara is to hear a cascade of words so true that you weep at the recognition. This book of sermons is no different. That she would share them with us means we will all preach more truthfully, write more incisively, and bear our souls to our God and our kin, knowing that this is the only way to create heaven on earth. With daring vulnerability in search of the holy inside each of us and all around us, Barbara leads the way."

—Jacqui Lewis, Senior Minister, Middle Collegiate Church, and
coauthor, *Ten Essential Strategies for Becoming
a Multiracial Congregation*

"Esteemed preacher, professor, and writer Barbara Brown Taylor is always a guest as a preacher, but in these pages, she is such a gracious homiletical host. Readers are guests at a gospel feast through her lucid, loving, honest, humble sermons. At this linguistic table, strangers will not only find a home in God but feast on a Word who is both a holy guest and holy host through the Holy Ghost. This book is so delightfully human and a fine example of homiletical hospitality at its best. Taylor's words are gifts of God for the people of God. They are verbal icons into the welcoming feast God has prepared for all. Thanks be to God!"
—Luke Powery, Dean, Duke University Chapel, and coeditor of the Connections lectionary preaching commentary series

"Barbara Brown Taylor is the master craftsperson of preaching—elegantly weaving the Bible, the news, humor, and storytelling in a way that leaves the listener both satisfied and changed. In a sermon on the parable of the Good Samaritan, she writes, 'Maybe it is a better idea to let our lives teach us what to believe instead of making our lives conform to our beliefs.' The disarming maybe hides a commandment, a truth of the nature of God revealed by the great preacher. This book is a beautiful chronicle of a traveling teacher, from graduation ceremonies to Sunday pulpits, inviting the reader to join her on the way."
—Winnie Varghese, Priest and Director, Justice and Reconciliation, Trinity Church Wall Street

"Barbara Brown Taylor never disappoints. As a collection of thirty-one Sunday sermons, delivered by a guest preacher, it's like a month of Sundays, perfect for just-before-going-to-sleep or with coffee and quiet time in the morning. Precise words, funny and profound turns of phrase, brilliant illumination of the gospel, and deep respect for those listening in the pews make this classic BBT!!"
—Bishop Gene Robinson, Vice President of Religion, Chautauqua Institution

Always a Guest

Always a Guest

Speaking of Faith Far from Home

BARBARA BROWN TAYLOR

WESTMINSTER
JOHN KNOX PRESS
LOUISVILLE · KENTUCKY

First edition
Published by Westminster John Knox Press
Louisville, Kentucky

20 21 22 23 24 25 26 27 28 29—10 9 8 7 6 5 4 3 2 1

Book design by Sharon Adams
Cover design by Barbara LeVan Fisher, www.levanfisherdesign.com
Cover art: © Jutta Kuss / Getty Images

Library of Congress Cataloging-in-Publication Data

Names: Taylor, Barbara Brown, author.
Title: Always a guest : speaking of faith far from home / Barbara Brown Taylor.
Other titles: Sermons. Selections
Description: First edition. | Louisville, Kentucky : Westminster John Knox Press, 2020. | Summary: "In this new collection of stories and sermons of faith, grace, and hope, Taylor finds that when you are the invited guest speaking of faith to people you don't know, you must seek common ground: exploring the central human experience"-- Provided by publisher.
Identifiers: LCCN 2020027859 (print) | LCCN 2020027860 (ebook) | ISBN 9780664261702 (hardback) | ISBN 9781646980093 (ebook)
Subjects: LCSH: Episcopal Church--Sermons. | Sermons, American.
Classification: LCC BX5937.T28 S47 2020 (print) | LCC BX5937.T28 (ebook) | DDC 252/.03--dc23
LC record available at https://lccn.loc.gov/2020027859
LC ebook record available at https://lccn.loc.gov/2020027860

PRINTED IN THE UNITED STATES OF AMERICA

∞The paper used in this publication meets the minimum requirements of the American National Standard for Information Sciences—Permanence of Paper for Printed Library Materials, ANSI Z39.48-1992

Most Westminster John Knox Press books are available at special quantity discounts when purchased in bulk by corporations, organizations, and special-interest groups. For more information, please email SpecialSales@wjkbooks.com.

Contents

Preface

On Being a Guest

When I left parish ministry twenty years earlier than expected, my preaching life was born again. This came as a surprise, since there was general agreement among my clergy friends that guest preaching was a lame gig. It was something people with no congregation did, filling in on a random Sunday for a preacher who was ill or away on vacation, or serving as a placeholder while a search committee did its job. It meant working hard on a sermon for people you did not know, but who knew each other well, which explained why it was so easy to make their eyebrows fly up when you said something that did not meet code, or pressed a bruise you did not know was there. Guest preaching was for people who didn't have a real preaching job.

Some of this was true. Once, when a charming clergy friend decided it would be fun for me to preach at his church while an assistant minister covered for me at mine, I failed to ask several important questions. Did he stand behind the pulpit when he preached or did he walk around? Did he use a manuscript when he spoke or did he look straight into people's eyes? How long were his sermons, usually? But even if I had remembered to ask, his answers would not have helped. Afterward, as I stood shaking hands at the door, a small woman with bright eyes and tan cheeks said, with genuine pity, "I'm sorry. It's just that we love Sam."

I tucked that wisdom away and pulled it out years later when I was always and only a guest. Always ask questions. Remember they love their pastor. Don't pretend to be something you're not. My real job was teaching college by then, which freed up my weekends for the first time in decades. Invitations came and I accepted them, learning to preach in a whole new way.

The first gift of guest preaching was the loosening of denominational bonds. I learned how to wait for the Spirit to move in a Pentecostal church, even if it meant the sermon started late and ended even later. I learned that thirty minutes was about right for Baptists and too long for Lutherans. I spoke in gymnasiums, under tents, on stages, and in cafeterias, without any familiar furniture or forms of worship. The disorientation was dazzling. None of my Episcopal lingo worked. I had to reach for language that lived closer to the heart of common Christian experience.

There were also invitations from college and university chapels, which caused me to test the age limits of my resources. Some of my favorite books were written when I was in college, which made them grandparent-age for a twenty-first-century sophomore. This worked fine with older congregations, but a chapel full of young people—even those required to be there—deserved a new review of culture and media. The gift of being their guest led me to discover new authors, musicians, bloggers, filmmakers, performance artists, and podcast hosts who woke me up to new ways of communicating with people of any age.

The most surprising gift was the freedom to preach without fear of being fired—or, if not fired, at least roundly criticized with apparent relish. Since I have been married to a churchgoer for a long time, I know that criticizing the sermon is a group sport that can be carried out with no real malice toward the preacher (though this distinction is often lost on the preacher). Being a guest doesn't prevent it from happening. The difference is that both my listeners and I know it's a one-shot deal, freeing us both to say and think things we might not otherwise have said or thought. Since someone responsible has invited me, I am presumably safe but still unpredictable, like the babysitter who shows up with steel darts and a dartboard instead of a Monopoly game. If all goes well, I might be invited back. If not, I won't. Either way, there's no lasting harm. The great thing about guests is that they go home.

What I value most about speaking of faith far from home is that I have to travel light. I don't know my hosts well. There are so many ways of being Christian that I don't even know for sure how the worship service will go. I certainly don't know who the pillars of the church are, or the troublemakers, or what kind of a week they have all had. I don't know what turns a stranger's speech into a sermon for them. I don't know what they depend on it to do. All of these uncertainties unpack my bags until there are only a few things left: a sacred text, a trust in the Spirit, an experience of being human, and the desire to bear good news.

All of these uncertainties unpack my bags until there are only a few things left: a sacred text, a trust in the Spirit, an experience of being human, and the desire to bear good news.

When I worry that won't be enough, I remember there may be another guest in the congregation that day—someone who didn't mean to come to church but turned in at the last minute, or came to placate a relative, or please a friend. They don't know the same things I don't know. They too are traveling light. They are starting where I'm starting, with the desire for something to happen this morning that will make a difference.

The only thing I know that the other guest may not know is that something does happen, over and over again, in the most surprising ways. Sometimes it's a praise dance and sometimes it's a descant by the choir on the last verse of a hymn. Sometimes it's a spontaneous baptism and sometimes it's an old couple holding each other up on their way to take Communion. I hate to say it, but it's rarely the sermon, at least not all by itself. Whether there's a guest in the pulpit or a pastor who knows everyone by name, that person's job is to do what any person sitting in front of them could do: give voice to the faith that is in them, and trust God to do the rest.

Chapter One

How to Live with High Anxiety

Luke 21:25–28

"There will be signs in the sun, the moon, and the stars, and on the earth distress among nations confused by the roaring of the sea and the waves. People will faint from fear and foreboding of what is coming upon the world, for the powers of the heavens will be shaken."

—Luke 21:25–26

Good morning, church. If you're visiting today, as I am, there are a couple of things you need to know right here at the start, because I'm your flight attendant and we're in for a bumpy ride. The turbulence is predictable, since there are two different weather patterns that always collide on the first Sunday of Advent.

The first is a happy high-pressure front. Today is New Year's Day for Christians—the first Sunday of the new church year—which sets our sights on the birth of the Messiah four weeks from now. Good news! The Christ is coming! It's time to get the nursery ready and reorder your priorities, because every urgent thing in your life is about to kneel before the one important thing that wants to be born anew in you: Emmanuel, which is to say: the God in you, the God in the person sitting next to you, the God with us, above us, below us, and among us, willing to be made known through us, and at the same time willing to become small enough to hold in our arms. This baby's on the way.

You'd expect champagne to be served on such a flight, but the happy high-pressure front is only one of the strong currents under our wings today. The other is a stormy low-pressure front, causing the captain to see strange things out the window. Christ is still coming, but in a cloud this time. Cabin service has been suspended due to the apocalypse, and we're all sitting in exit rows. You don't remember saying you would assist in case of an emergency? I'm afraid it's too late to change seats now. You, me, Emmanuel—we're all buckled in and we're all in this together. This morning's Gospel is our wake-up call, and it may take a while to hear the good news in it.

You just heard one version of it from Luke's Gospel. The backstory is that Jesus was in the Temple in Jerusalem. There were a bunch of people standing around, remarking on what a grand place it was, and how grand it was for them to be there. If it was anything like the Washington National Cathedral in DC, then the place was so packed with people trying to get a good angle with their selfie sticks that no one could see much of anything else. Or maybe it was the sheer size of the place that stunned them. The last time I was at the Cathedral, a guide told me you could lay the Washington Monument down the center aisle for an almost perfect fit. The place is that big.

Whatever version of that was going on inside the Temple, Jesus was irritated by it: the wealth, the splendor, the gawking. It all seemed so wrong to him that he decided it was the perfect teaching moment. Before people could head down to the gift shop for a souvenir postcard and talk about where to go to lunch, he said something loud enough for those standing around him to hear. Don't get too attached, he said, because it's all coming down (21:5).

Since it's easy to doze while you're listening to a familiar translation, here is another one from Eugene Peterson's The Message that may be different enough to win a fresh hearing. First, Jesus says,

"It will seem like all hell has broken loose—sun, moon, stars, earth, sea, in an uproar and everyone all over the world in a panic, the wind knocked out of them by the threat of doom, the powers-that-be quaking.

"And then—then!—they'll see the Son of Man welcomed in grand style—a glorious welcome! When all this starts to happen, up on your feet. Stand tall with your heads high. Help is on the way!" (Luke 21:25–28, MSG)

A few verses later, he continues:

"But be on your guard. Don't let the sharp edge of your expectation get dulled by parties and drinking and shopping. Otherwise, that Day is going to take you by complete surprise, spring on you suddenly like a trap, for it's going to come on everyone, everywhere, at once. So, whatever you do, don't go to sleep at the switch. Pray constantly that you will have the strength and wits to make it through everything that's coming and end up on your feet before the Son of Man." (vv. 34–36 MSG)

Earth and sea in an uproar. Global panic. The threat of doom. The powers quaking. I don't know about you, but I don't need much reminding about such things. I hear them on the radio every morning. I hear them on the news every night. I read about them on the front page of both newspapers that come to my house. I see them in the previews at the movie theater.

Earlier this week I was at a Catholic school of theology in San Antonio, where a professor asked if I had heard about the Hallmark explosion. Given some of the terrible things that have been in the headlines lately, I thought he meant an actual explosion.

"Oh, no!" I said, trying to think where Hallmark's headquarters were. "Was anyone hurt?" But he meant the *ratings* had exploded. Over the last two years, the Hallmark TV channel has zoomed to the top tier of cable channels with offerings such as *Love Comes Softly*, *In My Dreams*, and *Where the Heart*

Is. As different as these dramas are, what they have in common are happy endings. The characters in them do the right thing. Problems are resolved without anyone getting hurt. Sweethearts finally get together in the end. A month ago, Hallmark's network ratings surpassed CNN's. Now that December's here, the Christmas lineup will put Hallmark neck and neck with Fox and ESPN.

I totally get it. At my house, it's either *The Crown* or a frontier Western, depending on who gets to the TV clicker first. On *Longmire*, when Sheriff Walt finally exhausts all peaceful means and unholsters his pistol to let a bad guy have it, my husband, Ed, turns to me and says, "I'm sorry, but that guy needed to be dead."

We're living in scary times. With or without newspaper subscriptions, social media, and live streaming, it's hard to imagine anyone who can avoid the palpable anxiety that pervades our culture. It comes up in texts, in telephone conversations—even around dinner tables on nights out with friends. Something as slight as a see-through straw can conjure the image of the Great Pacific Garbage Patch, with its 79,000 tons of floating plastic. Mention the midterm elections during the appetizers and you'll be talking about the end of Western democracy by dessert.

There are a lot of ways people handle their anxiety, and the Hallmark Channel is probably the most benign. Shopping also works for some people; gin and sedatives for others. But since we're in a church this morning, there is good reason to return to the Gospel teaching for its clues to how Christians have lived with their anxiety from the start.

Best guess is that Luke's Gospel dates to the last decades of the first century, which means that he had lived through the end of his world a couple of times over—not just the crucifixion of Jesus, but also the executions of Peter, James, and Paul; the destruction of the temple in Jerusalem; Nero's persecution of the early church; and perhaps even the eruption of Mount Vesuvius in 79 CE, which rocked the ancient world with 100,000 times more thermal energy than the bombings of Hiroshima and Nagasaki combined.

Luke was not an eyewitness to *all* of these things. Like us, he got most of his headlines from a distance, but doomsday was not lurking somewhere in the future for him. It was past; it was present. It was the reality in which he wrote his Gospel, doing his best to set down the saving news of Jesus for those who were caught up in it too.

How did Jesus speak to their anxiety? Most importantly, I think, he did not tell them to cut it out. "People will faint from fear and foreboding of what is coming upon the world," he said. *Who could have known that better than him?* Terrible things happen, and you would have to be made out of metal instead of flesh to be fearless in the face of what might happen next. Jesus knew that. On one of the lowest nights of his life, he asked to be spared from what was coming next. "Father, if you are willing, remove this cup from me." At the same time, he knew that wasn't his call. "Yet, not my will but yours be done" (Luke 22:42).

This is a lifesaver: to know that the one we call Lord and Savior also knew fear and foreboding. He was made of tender flesh just like we are. Even he had to learn what could be changed and what could not. If his courage was superior to ours, it wasn't because he was anxiety-free but because he kept moving in spite of it.

He also knew that God was up to something that involved breaking before it involved mending, which means that the terrible things were not all coming from the enemy. That tumult Jesus was warning people about—uproar, panic, doom—it wasn't being caused by some malignant assault from the underworld, but by the gravitational pull of the kingdom of God drawing near. "Now when these things begin to take place," Jesus said, "stand up and raise your heads, because your redemption is drawing near" (21:28).

This is mind-bending for those of us who think we know what redemption looks like, who believe we are competent to judge whether something is coming from the enemy or from God. But there you have it: Jesus' lifesaving news is that our redemption is embedded in the things that cause us the greatest anxiety.

Jesus' lifesaving news is that our redemption is embedded in the things that cause us the greatest anxiety.

To go back to my flight metaphor for a moment, you might think about the last time you hit some really rough air—rough enough to make one of the overhead compartments pop open, maybe, or at least to make you grab your armrests and look around to see if anyone else looks as frightened as you feel. The minute you realize there is nothing you can do about any of this, your priorities can change fast. The humanity of the person in the seat next to you can become as precious to you as your own. Her survival can become inseparable from yours. Then the plane evens out and you both go back to reading your magazines. But I'll tell you what: there's nothing like some big-time turbulence to teach you how to pray. You can learn about what really matters to you in a moment like that, which has nothing to do with losing your luggage or making it to your next meeting on time.

Since Jesus isn't attached to the same things we are, he can take the God-view, which is about more than redeeming our individual lives. God means to redeem the *world*, which is going to require some major teardowns before the global renewal project can go forward. In this view there is some divine bulldozing to be done, some cosmic asbestos removal to be completed, before the world is safe for God's creation to live in again. All the systems, powers, and economies that keep us separated into first class and coach—they're already doomed. All the tribal politics that thrive on making us fear and loathe each other, every kind of religion that demonizes the stranger or violates the young—it's all coming down.

Jesus won't soften the message, but he does re-brand it. When you see these things begin to take place, he says, stand up and raise your heads, because your redemption is drawing near. That's not Satan coming in the cloud, or your most despised politician, or the mother of all hurricanes. It's him—the Son of Man—coming in power and great glory. If you can let that in—even a little—then you have opened the door for God to sanctify your anxiety.

The last thing Luke records Jesus as saying today is that it's really important not to let our worries make us check out. That's something else he knows about us—how likely we are to lie down when it's time to stand up, to cover our heads when it's time to raise them. When the turbulence gets really bad, it's tempting to retire from as much reality as you can. You know how it works. Lower the room-darkening shades and settle in for a full season of some world other than your own on your giant screen. Cover the bed with mail-order catalogs and empty pizza boxes. Do anything that works to take your mind off what's really going on.

Some people even use church to take their minds off reality, but none of us have come here for hot chocolate this morning. We have come for the kind of truth we're not getting anywhere else in our lives, and as hard as it may sometimes be to hear, Jesus promises it will save our lives—because the one who comes to us first as the Son of Mary in a manger comes again as the Son of Man in a cloud—not just once, but over and over again.

Luke thought the world was coming to an end in his time. Grave-diggers during the Black Plague were sure it was happening in theirs. Soldiers in the Great War thought they were living in the last days. During the last hours of 1999, millions of people prepared for doom as the clock swept toward Y2K. Maybe the end is always coming at us, in some form or another, so that every generation gets some practice at apocalypse before we pass away. That's what Jesus says, anyway. "Truly I tell you, this generation will not pass away until all things have taken place. Heaven and earth will pass away, but my words will not pass away" (21:32–33).

This is the heart of his teaching about how to live with anxiety. While everything else in heaven and on earth is bound to come to an end, his words will not. They will go on making sounds even if there is no one left to hear them. In the meantime, there is a deathlessness about them that holds out its hands to us, giving us a way to live even when we are scared to death.

"Love your enemies, do good to those who hate you, bless those who curse you, pray for those who abuse you. If anyone strikes you on the cheek, offer the other also; and from anyone who takes away your coat do not withhold even your shirt. Give to everyone who begs from you; and if anyone takes away your goods, do not ask for them again. Do to others as you would have them do to you." (Luke 6:27–31)

When the babe is born a few weeks from now, he won't be nearly that articulate. All he'll be able to do is cry for his mother Mary's milk, and maybe curl his fingers around one of Joseph's. But these words will be forming in him, along with many others, so that when he speaks them at last we will not only be able to hear them coming out of his mouth but also see them leafing out in his life—a way of life he commends to us too. It is the kind of life we can live in, through, and beyond the headlines, while we stand up—wide awake and full of purpose—to take part in the coming of God's reign at last.

Westminster Presbyterian Church,
Nashville, Tennessee
First Sunday of Advent
December 2, 2018

Chapter Two

Errors about Beauty

Matthew 6:25–33

"Consider the lilies of the field, how they grow; they neither toil nor spin, yet I tell you, even Solomon in all his glory was not clothed like one of these. But if God so clothes the grass of the field, which is alive today and tomorrow is thrown into the oven, will he not much more clothe you—you of little faith?"

—Matthew 6:28b–30

Good morning, everyone. Some of you are here because this is the last event listed in your Faith and Art Conference schedule.[1] Others of you are here because this is where you are on Sunday mornings, conference or not, which means that a few of you have given your regular seats to visiting strangers. In Christian tradition, this increases the likelihood that there are angels among us, though that is often difficult for adults to discern. If there are children sitting near you this morning, keep an eye on them. They almost always know who the angels are.

I am here because I was charmed by the invitation to come to a church that opens to the world in such a generous way. In a time when too many congregations are bent on self-preservation, it is rare to find one that actively seeks partnerships with people who do not belong to it—artists and scholars of many traditions and none, brought together by the common conviction that art is a friend of faith, not an enemy, and that the urge to create brings people together in ways that few other things can. In the biblical view, this is because human beings are made in the image of God. The Creator made us to co-create, and there is little that gives us as much pleasure as making beautiful things: not just paintings, poems, sculptures, and symphonies, but also gardens, cakes, perfect designs in new-mown grass, and babies. When we put something beautiful into the world, it is Genesis all over again. We are engaged in divine work.

This congregation knows that, but I wonder if you also know what a long road the arts have traveled to be welcomed back to church. That is what I want to talk about this morning—the rightful place of beauty in the life of faith, and why that has been such a hard case to make. I want to blame it on the Protestant Reformation, since there are so many differences between the "before" and "after" of that. Before the Reformation, the church was the richest and most reliable patron of the arts. Think of Chartres Cathedral, which kept sculptors, painters, and stained-glass artists busy for centuries. Think of Hildegard of Bingen, the twelfth-century abbess who was also an architect, playwright, musician, and composer. Think of Raphael, Michelangelo, Dante, da Vinci.

For the citizens of Geneva, at least, "after" began when John Calvin was called to the old Cathedral Church of Saint Peter in 1541 and started making changes. He and his followers soon emptied the church of its altars, paintings, statues, and furniture. I don't know why they left the stained glass, but they did. The great organ fell silent, since Calvin did not believe instrumental music had any place in Protestant worship. He disbanded the choir. He allowed the congregation to sing the psalms, since there was precedent for that in Scripture, but everyone had to sing them in unison, without accompaniment. Beyond that little bit of melody, and whatever color still filtered into the space through the old Catholic windows, there was nothing to distract people from the pure worship of God. In Calvin's view, the greatest art was the plan of God, and any art that detracted from that plan was the work of the devil.[2] Art for art's sake—art that aimed only to please the eyes or ears—was no more than an occasion for sin.

One thing I am not going to try to sort out for you this morning is the relationship between the beauty of creation (God's art) and the beauty of the arts (our creations). Though there is a lot to be said about what makes them alike as well as what makes them different, I am going to use the terms interchangeably—beauty and art—so we will all have something to think about later. Though Calvin had nothing nice to say about the human arts, he wrote at length about the beauty of creation, which he said is filled with "bright lamps" meant to show us the glory of God. The problem is that most of us content ourselves with looking at the lamps instead of what they are meant to show us. The problem is that we think chiefly of our own pleasure.

The problem is that most of us content ourselves
with looking at the lamps instead of what they
are meant to show us. The problem is that
we think chiefly of our own pleasure.

Calvin was not the first or last great thinker to worry about that, which is why I can't blame him or the Reformation for all the trouble between art and faith. More than a thousand years *before* Calvin, Plato worried that art fed the world of illusion. It kept people focused on the beautiful shadows dancing at the back of the dark cave instead of leading them out to engage true reality in the full light of day. Two hundred years *after* Calvin, the philosopher Immanuel Kant worried that our judgments about beauty are too wrapped up in our own self-interest. If there is anything universal about beauty, he said—if we are to find any common good in it—then we should be able to recognize beauty even in things that do not please us. Beauty should be able to lead us beyond the thumbs-up or thumbs-down of our own likes and dislikes. A hundred years after Kant, Tolstoy wrote two of the most famous novels of all time before he became a radical Christian in late middle life. After that happened, he dismissed both *War and Peace* and *Anna Karenina* as "bad art," since he had not created them with the will of God in mind.[3]

Whatever you think of all that, it is quite a lot of negative testimony about the ways that beauty and the arts can distract people from true faith. The arts tempt people to idolatry. The arts feed people's illusions. The arts thrive on self-interest, leading them to think of their own pleasure instead of pleasing God. Some of the most activist Christians I know might say it differently, but they too harbor a fear that beauty has the power to distract people from the work of justice. They may even be right. At the moment, I can think of a lot of people who say they feel closest to God in nature, and none at all who say they feel closest to God in a picket line at a refugee detention center. If justice has to be beautiful to get our attention, justice will suffer.

That's why I chose the passage from Matthew's Gospel for today—not because I knew it held the answer to the problem, but because I hoped it might reveal something about Jesus' own attitude toward beauty. The teaching comes near the end of his Sermon on the Mount. It is one of the most poetic things Jesus ever said. He gestures grandly in the direction of two of the most beautiful things on earth in order to make his point, which concerns the futility of human anxiety. "Can any of you by worrying add a single hour to your span of life?" (v. 27), he asks at the beginning. It's a rhetorical question. Of course we can't. "Therefore do not worry" (v. 31), he says at the end, which we can't seem to do either.

In between the question and the directive, he offers the example of worry-free birds and lilies for emulation, which has never struck me as remotely helpful. As much as I love watching chimney swifts grab their dinner from the air over my front yard at dusk, I cannot live on bugs. As much as I admire the wild iris that has just bloomed in the desert of last year's dead leaves, I don't have anything that color in my closet and it would not keep me warm if I did. Jesus' advice to handle my anxiety about the future by following the example of the birds of the air and the lilies of the field simply has not done it for me—until now.

It was a little book that popped me through—not by a spiritual writer but by a professor of aesthetics at Harvard named Elaine Scarry. She turned out to be the perfect foil for Plato, Kant, and Calvin. Her book is called *On Beauty and Being Just.* I bought it because of the lovely painting of bird eggs on the cover and because I had never seen beauty linked to justice in the title of a book before. It was not an easy read, either the first time or the second, but when her point became clear it rang my heart like a bell.

"Beauty prompts a copy of itself," she wrote. When you see something beautiful, it stops you in your tracks. It makes you want to replicate it somehow—draw it, write a song about it, tell someone about it. Yesterday I saw a cottage on Scotland Street in Dunedin that was so beautiful it would not let me walk past without stopping to admire it first. The front door was all but hidden by low boughs and flowering vines. The sidewalk was lined with flowers and folk art. There were bird feeders under the trees and bat boxes tacked to the tree trunks. I had to take a picture of it, though I don't have a Facebook page or Instagram account to post it on. I just had to make a copy of it, because it was too beautiful for there to be just one of it in the world.

So that was Scarry's first point. Her second point was that seeing beauty awakens the seer to what is *not* beautiful—specifically, to what has been injured, disfigured, cheapened, or debased. As the poet Wendell Berry once said, "There are no unsacred places; there are only sacred places and desecrated places."[4] To see a lily blooming in a field of fragrant grass is different from seeing a lily blooming in the ruins of a clear-cut forest, but the beauty of the one makes the beauty of the other all the more poignant. In this way, beauty is capable of moving people toward the hard work of repair—because once you have been touched deeply by beauty, in a lily or a human face, it is difficult to resist engaging the kind of justice that clears the way for more beauty in the world.

Scarry's third point is that beauty has the power to remove us from the center of the universe like almost nothing else can. It takes us out of ourselves in breath-taking ways. Christians may call this the power of "redemption" or "salvation." Artists and philosophers have called it the power of "de-centering" or "un-selfing." Whatever your word for it, it is what happens when you are stopped right where you are by beauty, when you give yourself over to it entirely, when you lose track of how much time you spend in the presence of it, when you come back to yourself changed by it—a little or a lot—so that your vision is expanded from that moment forward. You see more. You feel more. You *are* more. Paradoxically, the effect of un-selfing is that you emerge more connected to everything around you than you ever were before.

Last Wednesday I was walking back to my house from the mailbox—a nice three-minute walk along a split-rail fence separating the gravel driveway from the pasture—made more difficult on this particular day by trying to balance two packages from Amazon, two newspapers, and a small stack of bills in my arms. Don't ask me why it wasn't enough for me to be walking under a blue sky with a breeze blowing the leaves around, but it wasn't. First, I managed to open the bills from the power company and Visa without dropping either of the packages. Then I shifted the bills underneath the smaller of the two packages so I could tear it open while I was still walking, since I order so much from Amazon that I can never be sure what has just arrived. It was pen refills—four boxes full—which slid out of the bubble mailer and fell onto the gravel, praise God, because that was when I saw the hawk.

The big tweed-colored bird was feeding on something in the pasture, which was the only reason I saw it before it saw me—so large, so regal, so unexpected—that when it turned its head to look at me, I was afraid to breathe. We held each other's gaze for three seconds in perfect stillness. Then a breeze ruffled one of the newspapers in my arms and the bird took off, opening and closing its long wings like a pair of silver scissors. I tried to memorize everything about it so I could find it in one of my bird books later, as if naming the exact breed of hawk would somehow help me hang on to the beauty when it was gone. Why did I need to name a bird that had already renamed me? For just a moment there, my name did not match the one on the bills and Amazon packages. My name was Dumbstruck. My name was Behold!

"Look at the birds of the air," Jesus said. "Consider the lilies of the field." As moral as he was—as much as he cared about the blessedness of the poor, the welfare of widows, the healing of the sick, and the raising of the dead—he seemed to know that what anxious people most need is to get over ourselves for a moment, losing ourselves in the kind of beauty that loosens our grip on all the things we mistakenly think will keep us safe. *What will we eat? What will we drink? What will we wear?*

Beauty cannot answer those questions for us, but it can make them seem small in the presence of something so luminous, so unexpectedly lovely and generously given that we welcome its disruption: the silver wings of a bird, the purple throat of a lily. Beauty can hold our gaze for a moment of perfect stillness. Then, when it is done dismantling us, beauty can bring us back to ourselves with a wider gaze and a surer sense of connection to every living thing, ready to engage the divine work of creating more beauty in the world, more justice and true love.

Early in her book, Scarry raises a compelling question about beauty. Almost everyone can remember having made an error about beauty, she says. Something we once regarded as beautiful no longer is—or something we once viewed as incapable of beauty suddenly reveals itself to us. In her case, she said, "I had ruled out palm trees as objects of beauty, and then one day I discovered I had made a mistake."[5]

I think the mistake most of us make about beauty is that we expect it to be *pretty*—to please us with its proportions, its balance, its harmony, its rhyme. If those are your requirements, I doubt I will be able to talk you out of them, but they will definitely cut down on how much beauty you see. Because whether you're focused on the beauty of nature or the beauty of the arts, there is a lot of *terrible* beauty out there—a lot of tragic beauty, ruined beauty, beauty that has been hurt so badly it hurts you too. Once, after my husband and I had watched our first live Shakespeare play and everyone we cared about lay dead on stage at the end, he turned to me in the dark with tears running down his face and said, "Wasn't that *wonderful?*"

There are war photographs like that, and African American spirituals, and drawings by Jewish children who died in Treblinka before they turned twelve. There are stories Jesus told that never stop chewing at you because there is something *not quite right* about them, something higher than justice at work in them that leaves you wondering what righteousness has to do with love at all. These upsetting works of art are beautiful too, but not in the sense of pretty. They are beautiful in the sense of labor-and-delivery, in the sense of a white flag over a battlefield, in the sense of the first bird to land on the lifeboat with something green in its beak. You were lost. Then you were found, with beauty all around.

Before I leave you, let me point out that Jesus' directives to look at the birds of the air and consider the lilies of the field are phrased like commandments meant to save our lives. *Do look. Do consider.* In the Sermon on the Mount, they are snug up against other commandments such as, "Do to others as you would have them do to you" (Matt. 7:12), and "Do not store up for yourselves treasures on earth" (Matt. 6:19). If the teachings about the birds and lilies don't stick in the mind the same way the others do, that may be because we are still reluctant to value Jesus' instructions about beauty as much as we value his instructions about justice.

Yet all of these teachings come from the same Savior. If we can do what he says for a moment—if we can let ourselves be "unselfed" by considering the beauty of a hawk, a child's last drawing, a wild iris, a resonant lament—there is no telling what might happen next. Beauty might turn out to be so woven into the hem of the Savior's garment that we cannot reach out to touch it without being healed, then sent on our way to make more of it in the world. The only way to know for sure is to stop worrying for a moment and give it a try.

Palma Ceia Presbyterian Church,
Tampa, Florida
Fourth Sunday of Easter
April 22, 2018

Chapter Three

The Dominion of Love

Genesis 1:24–31; Matthew 5:43–48

Then God said, "Let us make humankind in our image, according to our likeness; and let them have dominion over the fish of the sea, and over the birds of the air, and over the cattle, and over all the wild animals of the earth, and over every creeping thing that creeps upon the earth."

—Genesis 1:26

If birds could write books, their story of creation would no doubt read quite differently than ours. In the first place, I expect they would make quite a lot out of that wind of God that swept over the face of the waters in the beginning of creation. When humans read "wind" we feel it on our faces, pushing our hair around and maybe even our bodies, but not many of us have a clue what it is like *not* to feel the wind because you are *in* it—moving at the same speed, in the same direction.

"The wind blows where it chooses, and you hear the sound of it, but you do not know where it comes from or where it goes. So it is with everyone who is born of the Spirit." (John 3:8)

Birds *love* that verse.

Sea creatures would probably still arrive on day five in the bird book of creation—pelicans would insist on that—plus, it makes sense to work your way up from the depths of the sea to the vaults of the heavens, filling creation with creatures as you draw nearer and nearer to God. On that ladder, land creatures would come next—mice, chipmunks, goats, humans, camels, things like that—earthbound creatures that could not get off the ground for more than a second or two without coming right back down again—hard—on all those *feet.*

Flying squirrels were pretty advanced at getting off the ground. Mountain goats were so-so, but people? It was pitiful even to watch them try—jumping off rocks, flapping their arms. Sometimes when they slept you could see their limbs twitching, as if they were dreaming of flight. None of this was their fault, of course. Bird mothers taught their children never to make fun of land creatures.

"God made them that way," they said, "the same way God made you. Now go outside and fly."

But day six! That was the day everyone got excited about when the book of creation was read in Bird Church, because that was the day God created birds in the divine image—sparrows, ravens, wood ducks, and hoopoes; whooping cranes, turtle doves, mockingbirds, and indigo buntings—all of them different and yet all of them alike, with two eyes, one beak, and those two marvelous *wings*—their daily assurance that they were made in the image of their Creator.

Human beings thought that assurance belonged to them alone, which was hard to figure when you heard them read from their *own* book. "Guard me as the apple of the eye; hide me in the shadow of your wings," they read (Ps. 17:8). "Be merciful to me, O God, be merciful to me, for in you my soul takes refuge; in the shadow of your wings I will take refuge, until the destroying storms pass by" (Ps. 57:1). "How precious is your steadfast love, O God! All people may take refuge in the shadow of your wings" (Ps. 36.7).

How could you read passages like that and not understand that God was most like a bird? But the birds understood that wings were not just God's *gift* to them; the wings were also God's *call.* Being made in the divine image meant it was the birds' job to look after the sea creatures and the land animals as God would look after them—especially the human beings, who seemed in particular need of help. So of course the birds were glad to do what they could—waking people up in the morning with their sweet songs, thrilling humans with their aerobatics, and pretending to like the gummy white bread the children fed them down by the lake. *Akh, akh.*

Sometimes, under special order from God, the birds made food deliveries of their own to humans in the wilderness. Ravens fed Elijah day and night for a while. A dove helped Noah figure out when it was safe to leave the ark and find food on dry land. A cloud of quail volunteered to become food themselves, when a bunch of people wandering in the desert said they were dying of hunger. The birds gave their lives to feed them—but really, what else are you going to do, when you are the only creatures in all of creation made in the image of God? You love as God loves, right? You love *what* God loves, because that's what your life is for.

I cannot tell you how many times I read the first chapter of Genesis before I noticed something new on day six. For years and years I believed that human beings had day six all to ourselves—you know, the pinnacle of the story, God's last, best word in the utterance of creation. With all lesser creatures out of the way, the sixth day finally arrived.

God ordered a kettle-drum roll, cleared the divine throat, and said, "Let us make humans in our image, according to our likeness (*Yes, yes, here we are at last!*); and let them have dominion (*Oh yes! Do let us have that!*) over the fish of the sea, and over the birds of the air, and over the cattle, and over all the wild animals of the earth, and over every creeping thing that creeps upon the earth (*Over the whole ranch, as far as the eye can see! This really is a wonderful book, don't you think?*)."

Then about six months ago I noticed for the first time that day six doesn't start with that verse. Day six starts two verses earlier, with the creation of land animals—cattle, to be exact. The text does not mention any other animals by name *except* cattle—twice in fact, along with unspecified creeping things and wild animals. So now all of a sudden, humans don't have day six to ourselves anymore. We're sharing it with *cows*, for God's sake, which I don't have anything against except that they are such dim bulbs, with such active salivary glands, that all they really do is eat grass. Couldn't God have started day six with *snow leopards*? What's wrong with *antelope*?

I understand how valuable cows were in the ancient world, like buffalo for Native Americans. A single animal could provide milk, meat, hide, and even dung for the fire. Cows are so sacred in India that killing them is out of the question. Anyone who does it on purpose may soon find out that cows rank higher than humans. Then there's the book of Jonah, with the best last line in the whole Bible: "And should not I spare Nineveh, that great city," God says, "wherein are more than sixscore thousand persons that cannot discern between their right hand and their left hand; and also much cattle?" (4:11 KJV).

Still, it's a real comedown to discover that humans share the sixth day of creation with *cows*. God may have made us for special purpose, but we did not have our own production date. We were made on the same day as cows and creeping things and wild animals of every kind. God may have given us dominion over them, but that didn't make us better than they were. According to the Bible, we were good, the same way everything else God made was good.

"God saw everything that he had made, and indeed, it was very good. And there was evening and there was morning, the sixth day" (Gen. 1:31).

In 1967, historian Lynn White wrote an article for *Science* magazine in which he charged that the roots of the ecological crisis are essentially religious. The problems derive from Christian tradition in particular, he said, which has taught people to view themselves as "superior to nature, contemptuous of it, willing to use it for our slightest whim."[1]

The Christian ethicist James Gustafson calls it "despotism"— one of the historical ways that people of faith have interpreted their divine right to dominion over the earth. In this view, you don't have to ask a tree before you bulldoze it for a subdivision. You just knock it down, push it into a pile with the corpses of other trees, and set it on fire. Then you are free to scrape the clear-cut earth free of green moss, tiny wild iris, unsuspecting toads, and a couple of thousand years' worth of topsoil before calling the pavers to come cover your artwork with steaming asphalt.

Oh—and if the mountain laurels block your view of the river, just cut them down too. The next time the river floods, the banks will collapse without those living roots; the river will silt up eventually, until you can push a sharp stick three feet straight down in the sandy bottom without ever hitting what used to be the riverbed, but what the heck—if the trout die, you can still buy some at the grocery store, already cleaned and boned, for just a few dollars a pound. You are lord over this playground, after all. God *said* so. It is all for you.

A lot has happened since 1967—so much that I don't hear many Christians sounding like despots anymore. The word I hear more often these days is "stewards." We are stewards of God's creation—not masters ourselves but divine servants, entrusted with caring for the vineyard until the master comes home. In this view, you can still build your subdivision, but you're going to save all the trees you can, planting two for every one you cut down, and at least covering the rudely exposed topsoil with wheat straw so that it doesn't blow away.

Why will you go to all this trouble, which will certainly cost you more money than despotism? Because the earth does not belong to you. It is on loan to you, like the talents in Matthew's parable. When the master comes home, you will be held accountable for what you have done with the earth, the sea, and all that is in them. There will be no hiding the waste dumps, the poisoned water, the floating fish, and bones of birds. "'Now when the owner of the vineyard comes, what will he do to those tenants?'" (Matt. 21:40).

"Steward" is an improvement over "despot," but it's still awfully utilitarian. A steward manages an estate, which likens the earth to a possession and links safekeeping to self-interest. The metaphor suggests that we don't care for rivers, fields, and skies because they are divine creations in their own right. We do it because we'll get in trouble if we don't, or because we need them to survive. We act from duty, not love, which may not be enough for this warming world of ours. We will not fight to save what we do not love.

We act from duty, not love, which may not be enough for
this warming world of ours. We will not fight
to save what we do not love.

That's why I want to keep scouring our tradition for more ways to conceive of our dominion over the earth, by which I mean our high privilege of being in relationship with creation in the same way that *Dominus* is in relationship with creation. Steward is good, but priest may be even better—someone who looks at the vineyard and sees more than low stone walls, hand plows, furrows, and seed sacks; someone who sees instead an altar laid with God's good gifts, just waiting for someone to bless them and hold them up to heaven again.

In 1923, sitting under a tree in the Ordos Desert of China, the visionary priest and paleontologist Pierre Teilhard de Chardin wrote his "Mass on the World," a long, mystical Communion prayer in which he celebrated the sacrament of the world. He did not have any bread with him in the desert (and no ravens brought him any). He did not have any wine either. He did not even have an altar, which is why he set his mass *on* the world. "I will raise myself beyond these symbols," he wrote, "up to the pure majesty of the real itself; I, your priest, will make the whole earth my altar and on it will offer you all the labors and sufferings of the world."[2]

Trusting that everything around him was the body and blood of God's Word, Teilhard held his empty hands in the air, consecrating the world to God and including himself in the bargain. It was a peculiar mass—scandalous, in the eyes of some—not only because the elements were unorthodox but also because there was nothing for the priest or anyone else to consume. Teilhard stood on the bread of the earth; he drank from the fiery chalice of the divine presence. In his celebration of Holy Communion, he lorded nothing over anyone; he used nothing up. His priestly dominion consisted of empty hands raised in blessing, as he offered the fruits of God's body back to God.[3] In this regard, his altar was the same one Jesus presided over at the hour of his death. There too the great high priest held up empty hands, his arms fixed in blessing, as he was lifted, along with the world he so loved, to God.

But here I am at a Presbyterian seminary, where the image of *priest* may leave some of Calvin's godchildren cold. How about *neighbor*, then? Neighbor will work, won't it? And who is my neighbor? (Where is Jesus when you need him to tell a story?) Do only two-legged ones qualify, or do my neighbors include the four-legged ones, the winged ones, the ones with fins and fur? Does God's compassion stop with human suffering, or does it extend to every creature in need of mercy, especially those with no voice of their own to cry out for help? Who will salve the wounds of the tree frog, the mountain laurel, the emperor penguin, the trout? We will not fight to save what we do not love. Meanwhile, God so loves us that not a sparrow falls to the ground without causing a shudder in the divine heart.

Just in case you missed the Associated Press announcement, the recipient of last year's VITA Wireless Samaritan Award was a seventeen-pound beagle named Belle. She was the first canine recipient of the award, given to those who use cell phones to save lives, prevent crimes, or help in emergencies. When Belle's owner, Kevin Weaver, suffered a diabetic seizure last summer, Belle saved his life by biting the 9 on his cell phone to dial 911. She was trained to do that, but she seems to have figured out all by herself how to read his blood sugar by licking his nose. If she senses anything out of whack, she paws and whines at him until he does something.

"Every time she paws at me like that I grab my meter and test myself," Weaver said. "She has never been wrong."[4]

I like *neighbor*, but *kin* may be even better. If you think about it, we are the latecomers to creation, we sixth-day creatures, who remain the youngest of God's children on the face of the earth. In Carl Sagan's famous example, if we could squeeze the creation of the cosmos into a single year, then the big bang happened on January 1. The sun and the planets came into existence on September 10, and human beings arrived on the scene at ten minutes before midnight on December 31. We are really late to the party, compared to algae, bats, dinosaurs, or salamanders.[5]

In the biblical account, our welcoming committee included "plants yielding seed, and fruit trees of every kind" (Gen. 1:11). It included "lights in the dome of the sky to separate the day from the night" (v. 14). It included "the great sea monsters and every living creature that moves," the ones with which the waters swarm "and every winged bird of every kind" (v. 21). And then of course there were the cows, made right before us, who stood around mooing while God laid us in the manger of the divine image, to have dominion over all of our elders on this planet.

What did the babies of creation do to deserve this? Nothing. And yet it is in us, at this late date, that the universe has become conscious. We are the first creatures to articulate the motion of the planets. We are the first to discern the commonality of all life. For those of us who believe God is the source from which we all arose, we are the first creatures to say so out loud. God may well prefer the sound of spring peepers, but I have to believe there was joy in heaven when the first human being looked at the sky and said, "Thank you for all this."[6]

Despots, stewards, priests, neighbors, kin. *Lovers* is my last shot, at least for today. We are made in the image of the First Lover, the divine one, who brought this whole shebang into being. If it is true that we have been put here to live in that image, then the only dominion we can possibly exercise is the dominion of love—without condition, without distinction, without self-interest or secret devotion to any other dominion, including the one in which the value of all things is reduced to their price.

"'You have heard that it was said, "You shall love your neighbor and hate your enemy,"'" God's Beloved taught. "'But I say to you, Love your enemies and pray for those who persecute you, so that you may be children of your Father in heaven; for he makes his sun rise on the evil and on the good, and sends rain on the righteous and on the unrighteous'" (Matt. 5:43–45).

In this sacred economy, there is one sun in heaven that shines on everyone and everything—no matter what genus or species they are, no matter how much saliva they produce, no matter what they have done or left undone. They all get sun. In the same way, when the rain comes down, everyone and everything gets refreshed—those who deserve it right along with those who do not, wings or no wings. That's just the way God is with God's creatures. We are here because God made us, and if God made us, we live by love. We are here to preside over the dominion of love in God's name. "'Be perfect, therefore, as your heavenly Father is perfect'" (v. 48).

What does perfection look like, in a warming world? Well, you know how it feels to take refuge under the shadow of the Great Bird's wings, don't you? It feels perfect, just perfect. So move over. Make room and spread your own wings wide, because there's a whole creation seeking refuge, and you—you're the spitting image of the One who gives life to all.

Columbia Theological Seminary,
Decatur, Georgia
April 16, 2007

Chapter Four

The Sacramental Sky

Genesis 15:1–6

*And Abram said, "You have given me no offspring, and so a slave
born in my house is to be my heir." But the word of the LORD
came to him, "This man shall not be your heir; no one but your
very own issue shall be your heir." He brought him outside and
said, "Look toward heaven and count the stars, if you are able to
count them." Then he said to him, "So shall your descendants be."
And he believed the LORD; and the LORD reckoned it to him as
righteousness.*

—Genesis 15:3–6

Before Abram became Abraham, he believed the Lord, and the
Lord reckoned it to him as righteousness. Here, in a single sentence, is the Old Testament version of salvation by faith alone.

It was the third time God had made promises to Abram. Abram
was not shy about reminding God that he still had no children.
When God reiterated the promise, Abram believed what God
told him, and that was all it took to make him righteous in God's
eyes. He did not have to fight any battles, follow any commandments, love any neighbors, or give anything up for Lent. All he
had to do was trust what God told him. So Abram did trust it, and
God reckoned it to him as righteousness.

Abram's wife Sarai was not part of this conversation, though she would have plenty to say about it later. Perhaps her husband had trust issues that she did not? Perhaps he had more energy for talking to God at the end of the day than she did. Whatever the reason, the story is about him, not her. It is about Abram—soon to become Abraham—the primal believer who did nothing to earn his righteousness in God's eyes. All he did was believe God's promises, and that was enough. Faith alone saved him.

Rewards followed in due time: first a son, then two grandsons, then a whole generation of great-grandchildren whose descendants would migrate to a land flowing with milk and honey. Would God have delivered those concrete goods if Abraham had not believed? We will never know. All we are told, in this testament and the next, is that those with faith the size of a mustard seed will be able to move mountains. They will be given what they ask for; the doors they knock on will be opened. Nothing will be impossible for them.

That is wonderful news for those who are sure they have faith. God bless you if you are one of them. I hope God agrees with you about your faithfulness in the end. Meanwhile, most of the people I know worry that they *don't* have faith, or not enough of it, or not the right kind. They keep their fingers crossed during parts of the Nicene Creed. They have a hard time with miracle stories. They are not *remotely* convinced that God loves them just the way they are.

They try hard to do what is right, but that isn't moving any mountains for them. It isn't even helping them sleep at night. They lie in the dark fretting about everything from where their teenagers are on Friday night to whether they will ever have enough money to retire. They wonder how many years they have left to get around to what really matters. They wonder who will die first, them or their partner. They hope they go first. Then they judge themselves for thinking like that. If they just had more faith, they tell themselves, if they just *believed*, then nothing would worry them.

In their minds, having faith means not being angry or afraid anymore. It means walking around with a compass inside of you that points true north no matter where you are. It means taking everything that comes to you with natural calm and confidence, because you are resting on the promises of God.

The great thing about Abraham is that he wasn't like that at all.

When God came to him for the third time, the first thing God said was, "Do not be afraid," which tells you that Abraham *was* afraid, or at least *prone* to being afraid. Who wouldn't have been? Sometimes, even when you have prayed holes in the rug for a word from God—announcing to the universe that you are as ready as you will ever be for some proof of divine life—sudden results can turn your bones to water.

Abraham may not have been all *that* afraid, because he changed gears pretty fast. "O Lord GOD," he said, "what will you give me?" (Gen. 15:2). That's such an embarrassing thing to say that you have to wonder why anyone wrote it down, but there it is. The Lord God came to Abraham and the first thing Abraham said was, "What will you give me?"

Of course, God had already told him that his reward would be very great, so the question was not off topic. It was just a little abrupt, a little short on front matter. When I was learning to pray, my teacher told me that you always begin by praising God. *Blessed are you, O Lord our God, King of the Universe. Holy is your Name, for you have done marvelous things.* Then you thank God for at least some of those marvelous things, even the ones that have not benefited you directly. *We thank you for the beauty of the earth, the gift of life, and the mystery of love.*

Then you may ask for what you want, but reverently and respectfully. You don't just say, "What will you give me?" (even if that's what you're thinking), or register a direct complaint like Abraham did. "'You have given me no offspring, and so a slave born in my house is to be my heir.'"

But that's what Abraham said, and God did not strike him dead. Instead, God reassured him. No slave would be his heir, God said. No one but a child of Abraham's own body would be his heir. Then God brought the old man outside, which means that he was inside before that—in a tent, maybe, where all he could see above his head was black tarp with a few rips in it.

Outside, Abraham could see a lot more than that. I don't know where you live, but chances are that none of us can see half of what Abraham saw. At the very least, there are three neighbors who leave their porch lights on at night. At worst, there are parking lots, football stadiums, tall buildings, and billboards all beaming so much artificial light at the sky that you might as well be in a tent for all you can see of the stars at night.

But Abraham could see—not just specks of light in the sky but the actual colors of the stars—some yellow, some red, some flashing back and forth between blue and green—plus millions of tiny ones so small they looked like phosphorescent clouds. There were triangles of stars up there, long rectangles of stars, swirls and rivers of stars up there.

"Count them if you can," God said, but even Abraham knew that was pure rhetoric. There was no way to count the stars. They went on and on, and not just that. They went deep and deep. If anyone had looked into Abraham's eyes right then, they would have seen them littered with stars, as many as would fit on the twin planets of one old man's eyes.

"So shall your descendants be," God said. And Abraham believed the Lord, and the Lord reckoned it to him as righteousness.

What made Abraham believe? We get all kinds of other details in this story, right down to the name of Eliezer of Damascus, but at the golden hinge of the story, the point at which the whole history of three major world religions could have gone either way, all we get is a flat statement of fact: Abraham "believed the LORD." *Since? Because?* If we are supposed to follow his example, could we have a little more information, please? Was the tipping point intellectual or intuitive? Did it require huge effort on Abraham's part, or was it as easy as falling in love? *How did Abraham come to faith in God?*

The story does not say. It just shows us what happened without telling us why, which is really very wise. If the story had given us a magic formula, we might have believed in the formula instead of the relationship between God and Abraham. We might have believed we had to do things in a certain way to get a certain result, but the story does not work that way. It just asks us to come out from whatever tarp we're under and look up at the sky, as God invited Abraham to look up at the sky. Then it leaves the rest to us.

The story does not work that way. It just asks us to come out from whatever tarp we're under and look up at the sky, as God invited Abraham to look up at the sky. Then it leaves the rest to us.

One of the most obvious details left out of the story is a proper definition of faith. Does it mean surrendering to God's will, or does it mean taking an active role in God's future? Does it mean accepting what you have been told without asking any questions, or does it mean wrestling every night with all kinds of scary angels? Does one always take a leap of faith, or does one some-times lurch toward faith instead? What happens inside a person that allows him or her to trust God?

I used to think that in order to trust anyone or anything I first had to determine the trustworthiness of the person or the thing. Before trusting a rickety-looking bridge to bear my weight, I waited until someone else my size walked across it first. Before trusting a friend to keep a confidence, I paid attention to whether or not she told me other people's secrets first.

This struck me as a logical way to proceed, and it worked well enough for a long time.

The only problem was that my ability to trust hinged on something outside of me that was beyond my control. If the bridge wobbled, I couldn't trust it. If the friend gossiped, I couldn't trust her. It was like my trust was not mine to give. It always depended on how someone or something else acted, so I was never really in charge of my own ability to trust. Like a day trader in the stock market, I might extend trust and withdraw it ten times a day—all depending on how the rest of the market was responding to my investment.

Then someone offered me a definition of trust that turned my logic upside down. "Your ability to trust doesn't have anything to do with anyone but you," he said. "You weigh the risks, then you decide. Basically, trust means deciding you can handle it if you get screwed."

He was right. Trust is never entirely logical. Faith never makes perfect sense. It is more like a gift that human beings are able to give—an act of ridiculous courage in which people who cannot control the outcome of their decisions to trust decide to trust anyway. They decide to act *as if* the universe were trustworthy, and they figure they can handle it if they get let down.

If today's story is any indication, things don't suddenly improve once you believe God. *You* don't suddenly improve. Abraham was as fearful and cranky *after* he believed God as he was *before* he believed God. There was that lovely moment in between while he was looking at the stars, but if you read one verse past where we stopped today, God promised Abraham some land and Abraham said, "'Oh Lord GOD, how am I to know that I shall possess it?'" (v. 8).

Here we go again.

But God didn't say, "I thought you believed me." God just told Abraham to go find a heifer, a goat, a ram, a turtledove, and a pigeon, maybe thinking that would keep the old man busy for a while. When Abraham had fetched them all and brought them back, he cut everything but the birds in two and laid the halves against each other.

God did not tell him to do that part, incidentally. Abraham already knew that was how you sealed a covenant in those days, the ancient equivalent of "Cross my heart and hope to die, stick a needle in my eye." Once you made your vows, you walked between the pieces of the slain animals, as if to say, "May the same thing happen to me if I fail to keep my word."

But Abraham fell into a deep and terrifying sleep before he could walk anywhere. The stars disappeared while God showed him the future of his starry descendants—how they would become aliens in a land not their own, where they would endure slavery and oppression for hundreds of years before emerging with great possessions. God even showed Abraham his own death. Talk about a rickety bridge.

When the old man woke up, he saw a smoking fire pot and a flaming torch pass between the pieces of meat he had laid out earlier, but there was nobody holding either one of them. There were just the smoke and the fire, God's favorite calling cards.

In this way, Abraham learned that God was taking the walk Abraham thought was meant for him. Abraham did not cross his heart that starry night. God crossed God's heart. While Abraham lay watching, God assumed the whole risk of the covenant, which included the very great risk of trusting Abraham with the divine promises and being wrong about him. So that is what faith looked like on one momentous night at least: God decided to believe, and Abraham accepted the risk of gambling on a God who was willing to gamble on him.

That may not be enough for you, especially since the rewards can be such a long time coming, with such hardship in the middle, and no guarantee that you'll sleep better even after they do. But if there is anything about this story that sounds true to you, then it is your story and you may step into it any time you want. You may leap or you may lurch. You may invent a whole new way of getting there, or not. But if you do, imagine this: a brand-new star will appear in Abraham's eye, as he gladly starts counting all over again.

Duke University Chapel,
Durham, North Carolina
Second Sunday of Lent
February 28, 2010

Chapter Five

Paralyzed by Polarization

Matthew 9:1–8

"For which is easier, to say, 'Your sins are forgiven,' or to say, 'Stand up and walk'? But so that you may know that the Son of Man has authority on earth to forgive sins"—he then said to the paralytic—"Stand up, take your bed and go to your home." And he stood up and went to his home. When the crowds saw it, they were filled with awe, and they glorified God, who had given such authority to human beings.

—Matthew 9:5–8

Dear graduating class of 2018: I am here at your invitation and could not be happier to answer your call. Right now it is hard for me to imagine a more inspiring group of people, both personally and professionally. You are my space explorers, my doctors without borders, my small organic farmers, and church whisperers— willing to go where few are willing to go, for low pay and high risk, on the off chance that you might be able to do a little good.

I had so hoped to talk to you about truth or beauty today, but I'm afraid it's going to be politics instead—or at least the politics of polarization, which is affecting so many of our congregations that it is impossible for me to ignore in your presence. Ninety-four percent of you are headed into parish ministry. One hundred percent of you care about the church, which means that every one of you will engage the politics of local congregations that are trying to figure out what it means to be Christian in our time.

A lot of them are really jumpy about it, too. Words that were not always loaded are loaded now. People who were not always defensive are defensive. Some are careful where they sit so they don't have to pass the peace with identified antagonists. Others hear things in sermons that are not there, posting them on social media before the preacher even sits down. In buildings with central aisles, a visitor might be forgiven for noticing that there is a left side and a right side, and that most people come in knowing exactly where they are going to sit. Christians of all kinds are taking the habits of the culture to church, and this is not going especially well for us. There are so many topics off the table right now that pretty soon we'll be talking to each other at coffee hour the same way we talk to taxi drivers.

"This is really some kind of weather, isn't it?"

"Traffic just seems to get worse and worse."

In light of today's Gospel, this kind of paralysis is one of the most difficult to heal, since it's so hard for those who suffer from it to admit that we need help. *My sins are forgiven? I'm sorry, sir, but you have the wrong pallet. You're looking for that person over there.* We all know we're wounded. Our sense of personal injury is one of the few things we have in common, but that only makes our stuck-ness worse, at least if we're waiting for someone else to make amends before we agree to move. When they don't, or won't, acknowledge our sense of being wronged, the venom that rises in the throat can be startling, especially for a Christian.

Two years ago I savaged a young relative of mine when he started ragging on my failed presidential candidate. We had never had any reason to lay down rules of engagement before. We had never had any practice. In the heat of the moment, the imbalance in power never even occurred to me. I just blew up. When I had finished twirling my fire batons at him, it was hard to say who was more burned. He seemed unable to move. I seemed unable to apologize. *I was there when this boy was born*, I thought. I was there when he made Eagle Scout, when he graduated from high school dressed like a Jedi knight, and still I was ready to rip him for his politics. If I couldn't do better than that, wasn't it time to give Jesus my resignation?

It was at a family dinner table and not a church. I was in jeans and not vestments, but I'm not sure that matters. What matters is that like a lot of Christians, I have a hard time with conflict. I have learned to view it as un-Christlike, which means that I know how to avoid it, deny it, sublimate it, and internalize it, but not how to enter into it with other people without feeling like a sinner.

"Love your enemies and pray for those who persecute you." (Matt. 5:44)

"If anyone strikes you on the right cheek, turn the other also." (v. 39)

"So when you are offering your gift at the altar, if you remember that your brother or sister has something against you, leave your gift there before the altar and go; first be reconciled to your brother or sister, and then come and offer your gift." (vv. 23–24)

Sometimes I think Jesus said things like that because he never pastored a church. Paul pastored churches, which is why I like his iteration better. "Bless those who persecute you," he told the Romans, "bless and do not curse them" (12:14). See? He knew about the cursing. "If it is possible, so far as it depends on you, live peaceably with all" (v. 18). *If it is possible. So far as it depends on you.* That was written by someone who had been through a conflict resolution process with his vestry, who knew that nothing you did was going to make your critics go away—and even if it did, their fresh replacements would arrive first thing the next morning.

Sometimes I think Jesus said things like that because he never pastored a church. Paul pastored churches, which is why I like his iteration better. "Bless those who persecute you," he told the Romans, "bless and do not curse them" (12:14). See? He knew about the cursing.

But note this: even Jesus' teachings take conflict for granted. You can't love an enemy if you don't have one. You can't turn *this* cheek if no one slaps *that* one first. While plenty of ordinary Christians believe that Jesus' teachings forbid conflict or require us to absorb it, the very existence of the teachings tells us that he knew conflict would be a regular part of his followers' lives, and that they needed to know they had choices about how to handle it. Otherwise they would only be able to find two gears: idle or attack.

A couple of weeks ago, when I was still hoping to talk to you about truth and beauty, the spring edition of *Reflections* arrived in my mailbox. It's a journal published by Yale Divinity School, my alma mater, which always focuses on one topic from a variety of perspectives. This time the topic was "confronting our divisions," and the perspective that changed mine came from a Presbyterian pastor in Arizona named Wes Avram.

He used to believe that dialogue was the answer to conflict, he said. If people of good faith would just come together across their differences, as ready to change their own minds as they were to change the minds of others, they could clarify their irreconcilable differences in ways that were not damaging to each other and renew their covenant to go forward together. They could look upon their temporary breakdown in the conflict lane as inevitable but fixable, allowing the spirit of reconciliation to get them back on the road.

He really believed that, he said. Then he went into the ministry.

The title of his article was "Stop Resolving Conflict!" and his thesis went like this: since conflict is inevitable—since it belongs to the human condition, and no one has ever found a permanent fix—why not stop treating conflict as a *breakdown* and start treating it like *standard procedure* instead? That way churches could stop pouring so much energy into making it go away (never going to work) and redirect the dream of *resolving* conflict to *normalizing* conflict. The new dream would be to build more productive *conflicted* communities that hold people together with higher ethical standards of engagement than the dominant culture ever will.[1]

If you're underwhelmed, that's because "the ministry of productive conflict" is never going to sound as good as "the ministry of reconciliation." But it's not like you have to choose between the two. I'm not even sure they're so far apart, if reconciliation means bringing people back together again instead of getting people to agree with each other again. *Again?* When have church people ever agreed about anything for longer than a couple of weeks at a time?

Sometimes I think the reason we talk about reconciliation so much is because we have managed so few lasting results in that department. I also think there's a secret part of us that shies away because reconciliation implies giving up some of what we want. That might make sense when the conflicts are prideful or petty, but what about when they're noble? Some of our conflicts are too important to give up on, even in the name of unity. Some of them are worth staying in the ring to fight, even if we're the ones who go down for the count. I mean that metaphorically, of course, given Jesus' teachings on nonviolence—though he was not exactly what you would call conflict-averse.

He tangled with the scribes and Pharisees. He threatened the money changers. He fought with his own disciples, especially Peter, more than once. He quarreled with his own mother. ("'Woman, what concern is that to you and to me?'" [John 2:4].) Read from a certain perspective, the gospel *requires* conflict to unfold—not just with enemies but also with family and closest friends—as Martha criticized Mary, Paul fought with Peter, and Barnabas split from Paul. How much shorter would the New Testament be if the churches in Corinth and Galatia had been more tranquil places? If the apostles and elders had not met in

Jerusalem to argue about whether to include Gentiles in their mission, would we be here at all?

It's not just that conflict is inevitable and some fights are worth having; it's that conflict is one of the ways God gets most deeply to us—not always, and never in the most pleasant way—but when people figure out that unity is about more than agreeing with each other and reconciliation has more to do with staying in the room than with winning—then remarkable things can happen. Two sides can discover a third way. People can see facets of each other they never saw before. Sometimes they can even say good-bye to each other without making anyone wrong. You know this is true because you have been there yourself—when the break-down became a breakthrough, and the Spirit got to you in the way you least expected.

So a part of your heart broke too? Here's some truth and beauty for you: that's how it works. You set out to change someone else and you are changed instead. You get all ready to defend yourself and you get forgiven instead. I wish it happened more often. I wish it had happened differently with my young relative, but this is very difficult work, especially for Christians, and we need all the help with our paralysis that we can get. But the dream is not to stay out of conflict.

The dream is to remember who we are and what matters most to us in the midst of conflict, to hold ourselves to higher standards of engagement with one another than the culture in which we live, and to love each other in ways that mystify our neighbors, on the off chance that it will do a little good.

This will take practice. This will take crazy confidence in the Spirit. Above all, this will take leaders like you, who are so brilliantly equipped to make a difference in the world. However you decide to do it, thank you for inviting me to be with you today, you church whisperers. You are my heroes, and I wish you all the best.

Virginia Theological Seminary,
Alexandria, Virginia
May 17, 2018

Chapter Six

What's Your News Source?

Matthew 6:25–32

"Therefore I tell you, do not worry about your life, what you will eat or what you will drink, or about your body, what you will wear. Is not life more than food, and the body more than clothing?"
—Matthew 6:25

There is no place on earth I would rather be this evening than here with you. You don't get many big passages in life, and this is one of them. In less than an hour, you will cross over from being students at Eden Seminary to being alumni of Eden Seminary, from being promising degree candidates to being graduates with extra initials after your names, from being people who came here looking for wisdom to being the people other people look to for wisdom.

But first you have to sit here, which is something else you don't get much of in life. You don't get many chances to hold still the way you are holding still right now—between one act of your life and the next, between the dreaming and the coming true. This ritual pause forces many people into an unnatural state of rest, so if you are feeling a little jumpy right now, a little like your head might be about to explode, that could be one of the reasons why. You are getting too much oxygen. You are missing all of your

41

usual distractions. You are not busy, for once, which has put you into a rare state of availability to the Spirit that eludes you when you have everything under better control.

I wish this meant that you are feeling invincible right now, but my guess is that most of you are feeling a little fearful instead. Actually, that's not a guess. It's more like a field report, since I have spies in the house tonight—five of you who took time out of the final weeks of this semester to tell me what you will miss most about Eden, how your vision of ministry has changed during your time here, and what you most need to hear as you go forth.

A number of things became clear while I sat with your answers. It is clear, for instance, that Eden is succeeding at being a welcoming, inclusive, and ecumenically diverse community. This is a place safe enough for your understanding of the world to be broken open, where your raw honesty and true presence are not just allowed but required. It is also clear that Eden has equipped you to serve in a wide variety of ministries, and not just the ones you had in mind when you came here, either. The Spirit has spun some of you around so that you are heading in another direction altogether, while others of you have discovered that ministry is not something you are being called to do *for* God's people but *with* them.

What became most clear, however, is that you have read the news. You know all about church decline, congregational conflict, and clergy isolation. You are fully aware of climate change, war in the Middle East, the shallowing of American culture, and the high cost of a global economy that depends on over-the-top consumption and leaves too many people out. Because you have gone to school fourteen miles from Ferguson, you have not been able to maintain the illusion that police don't kill unarmed teenagers, or that they do it somewhere else. Plenty of you have been *in* the news on that one, witnessing to the truth that Black Lives Matter and that even when nonviolent resistance does not work the way you want it to, it is still the Way of Life.

Because you know all of this, it is no wonder that some of you are feeling a little fearful on the eve of leaving Eden. With all that is going on in the world right now, who's going to believe your good news? Who's even going to *hear* it, between the clamor of yesterday's headlines about the death toll in Nepal and tomorrow's about how much money *Mad Max: Fury Road* is expected to earn this weekend? Sorry. I know. I'm only making it worse. But that's what happens when you let the headlines tell you what the world is like. Words such as "hopeless," "helpless," and "endless" come readily to mind. Words such as "broken," "chaos," and "decline."

A few years ago, a friend and I were talking about the most recent attempt at a peace deal in the Middle East—arguing about it, really—when he said, "Where did you *hear* that?"

"NPR!" I said.

"You mean National Propaganda Radio," he said.

"Well, where did you hear that thing you said?" I said.

"Fox," he said.

Once we let that sink in, we wondered what would happen if we tried listening to each other's news sources from time to time, because we really liked each other. We couldn't figure each other out, but we really liked each other. So it seemed worth a try, to eavesdrop on the other person's news source and see how that changed the conversation. I don't know if he tried, but I tried, once, for about three minutes. I couldn't do it longer than that. It was too disorienting. It was like turning on the radio to discover that I had been transferred to another planet—or worse yet, that I was an alien on my *own* planet. I simply did not recognize the world that was being described to me on my friend's channel.

That's when I decided it was really, really important to pay attention to where I was getting my news, because what showed up in that constant, repeating news cycle—along with the meaning that reporters, anchors, and guest experts made of it—was going to shape my view of the world more than any other source closer to hand: more than the Bible, more than what was happening in my own community, my own church, my own yard. If I continued to let the headline news run like white noise in the background while I washed dishes, drove my car, and worked out at the gym, then no one would have to bother trying to convince me that the world was hopelessly broken, because that conviction would already be at work (subliminally, without a single confirmation hearing), guiding my decisions about what was worth doing, believing, hoping—and what was not.

In the middle of the last century, when it became clear that the Nobel Prize–winning poet Czeslaw Milosz was about to be exiled from his native Poland, he visited friends in northern California, where he would later become professor of Slavic languages and literature at the University of California, Berkeley. In 1960, he wrote his friend Thomas Merton, the noted monk and writer, about the visit.

> I feel the heavy illness of American society is closely connected with "mass media." One should look for its roots there. . . . My children were looking for hours at television, to my impotent rage. This is a great responsibility to expose one's children to such influences—most often imperceptible to them—and to make decisions, as my decision of coming here, which risk distorting their lives. Just a few minutes before the television for me were enough to induce a state of shame and sadness for the whole evening. . . . It seems to me that America is bursting with talents and intelligence, but minds are turning round in a sort of spellbound dance of paralytics. The awakening is inevitable— but when and what awakening? As to myself I know I can disintegrate completely if I do not keep my thinking clear and hot.[1]

Milosz tried to talk Merton into leading a broad protest against commercial television, convinced that it was the root cause of both intellectual and political paralysis in the U.S. "Here we encounter the most thorny problem of democracy," Milosz wrote in a letter to Merton, "—if in every man is a sage and an idiot, whoever flatters the idiot wins."[2]

Fifty years later, it seems clear that Milosz had a point. Never mind *Here Comes Honey Boo Boo* and the *Real Housewives of Orange County*. Ask any news reporter what has happened to network news. Ask what kinds of stories journalists are being assigned to cover in order to keep viewers immobilized in front of their screens. At the same time, concede that television is here to stay—along with Facebook, Twitter, Tumblr, and Instagram—which makes it all the more important for us to find ways to keep our thinking clear and hot, to appeal to the sage and not the idiot, both in ourselves and in the communities we serve.

It can take a lot of work to round out the news. Did you know that on the same day a suicidally depressed pilot crashed a Germanwings airplane in the French Alps, killing all 150 people on board, an Arizona woman named Debra Jean Milke was released from prison after twenty-two years on death row when her conviction was overturned?[3] That same week, a judge in upstate New York dismissed all charges against forty-two people arrested for protesting plans to store millions of barrels of fracked petroleum gases in old salt caverns under the largest store of freshwater in the state. After making his judgment "in the interests of justice," Judge Raymond Berry told protestors he was proud of them. "You had a cause," he said, "and you fought it to the best of your ability."[4]

That same week the Sacramento City Council voted to allow farming on inner-city lots, freeing local residents intent on "transforming the 'hood for good'" to work together to improve food security in urban areas.[5] The FDA responded to a mandate from Congress to speed up its drug-vetting process, approving ten new drugs during the first three months of the year that promise to change the way advanced breast cancer, melanoma, and heart disease are treated.[6] Oh, and 115 babies were born that same week in Tulsa, Oklahoma—fifty-six boys and fifty-nine girls, including one set of twins.[7]

Does any of that make up for a single life lost in the French Alps? Of course it doesn't. Good news doesn't neutralize bad news. That's not the point. The point is that those two kinds of

> Good news doesn't neutralize bad news. That's not
> the point. The point is that those two kinds of news
> live closer together than most of our news sources
> would have us believe.

news live closer together than most of our news sources would
have us believe.

In my hometown of Clarkesville, Georgia, Sheriff Joey Ter-
rell was one of twenty community leaders who recently took
part in a homegrown version of *Dancing with the Stars* to raise
money for victims of domestic violence. He and his partner
didn't win, but everyone who watched them knew why Ter-
rell's shoulder might have seemed a little stiff that night. A
month earlier, he had been shot while responding to a domestic abuse call on 911. When he learned that a former deputy
of his was involved in the dispute, he went himself instead of
sending someone else. He hoped that he might be able to talk
the officer down, but he arrived too late. When he got there,
the deputy had already killed his ex-wife and her new boyfriend
while the deputy's daughter hid inside the house. It was the
worst possible news.

A month later, there was more news: "Dancing for the Stars
for Hope" was a sellout, with more than 650 people packed into
the Habersham Central High School gym. The benefit brought
in more than $64,000 in a single night—in a county where 21
percent of the population lives below the poverty line and the
median income is $39,000. Clearly, some people emptied the
cookie jar to be there. This enabled a local group called Circle
of Hope to continue providing emergency shelter, legal advo-
cacy, counseling for abused women and children, and community
education programs. Will that bring the former deputy's ex-wife
and her boyfriend back? Will it stop domestic violence? No, it
won't—but it kept people from feeling paralyzed, if just for a little
while. It moved the needle from "hopeless" to "hopeful," for one
night at least. That's good news.

Whatever kind of ministry you're headed into after tonight, you're about to become a news source in your community. You're about to become one of the people other people look to for wisdom about what is happening in the world—someone who can help them walk the swinging bridge of fully informed faith over a twenty-four-hour news cycle of paralyzing fear, helping them figure out what to focus on so they can manage their anxiety and distraction long enough to help someone else across. You'll have to be a really good reporter to do it, too, but after your time here, I'm confident you have the skills.

You know how important it is to follow the small stories as well as the big ones, for instance. You know that sitting down with someone for whom your language is a second language and doing some deep listening about how things look through their eyes can do more to change your worldview than reading the front page of the *New York Times*. You know that people waiting to see a doctor in an emergency room at St. Louis Children's Hospital have as much to teach you about what it means to be human as people waiting in a makeshift clinic halfway around the world.

You know how laughter can bubble up in the grimmest places—a knock-knock joke in a holding cell, a terrible pun in the middle of a street protest—everyday proof that how good or bad the news sounds depends a lot on us.

You also know more Bible stories than you did when you came here, don't you? That means you are now equipped with some truly paradoxical storylines about how the younger surpass the elder, the smaller outfox the larger, the crooked outshine the straight, and the loser pops up at the head of the line. Stories like that don't only happen in the Bible. Once you get the hang of them, they start showing up all over the place, just waiting for the right reporter to come along and get the news out.

Oh, and don't forget all that gratuitous beauty out there—birds that sing in spite of the unemployment rate, lilies that unfurl their ravishing petals as if they had never heard of climate change. For all the times that people say, "What did I do to deserve this?" when something terrible happens, I can't remember anyone saying the same thing when something gorgeous happens. The next time you're driving home after dark and you see a full moon coming up through the trees like a wide golden eye, please pull over, open your window, and yell, "Why did this happen to meeeeeeeeee?"

Mentioning such things in the news can earn you some scorn, I'm afraid. I don't know when we decided that the worst news is more serious than the best news, but we did. On the whole you'll get more respect if you dwell on the bad news, though I suspect that's because it gives your listeners a reason for staying paralyzed with anxiety. Still, you don't want to be a Pollyanna. You don't want to say, "'Therefore I tell you, do not worry about your life, what you will eat or what you will drink, or about your body, what you will wear. Is not life more than food, and the body more than clothing?'"

You don't want to say, "'So do not worry about tomorrow, for tomorrow will bring worries of its own. Today's trouble is enough for today'" (Matt. 6:34). The great news is that you have a direct source for that. You can just quote him and let *him* take the heat.

I don't know what your big stories will turn out to be, but you have everything you need to produce them—natural gifts, learned skills, keen mentors, sage hearts—and the ace reporter of all time at your back, reminding you to look high and low for the saving news in this world of crash victims and newborn babies, deadly injustice and dismissed charges, crazy violence and improbable kindness.

For the God who loves it all has given it all to you to love as well.

Eden Theological Seminary,
Webster Groves, Missouri
May 15, 2015

Chapter Seven

The End Is (Always) Near

Mark 13:14–23

*"But when you see the desolating sacrilege set up where it ought not
to be (let the reader understand), then those in Judea must flee to
the mountains; the one on the housetop must not go down or enter
the house to take anything away; the one in the field must not turn
back to get a coat. Woe to those who are pregnant and to those who
are nursing infants in those days! Pray that it may not be in winter.
For in those days there will be suffering, such as has not been from
the beginning of the creation that God created until now, no, and
never will be."*

—Mark 13:14–19

I imagine at least some of you are here this morning because you
were hoping to take an hour off from the headlines. It's not that
you don't care. Most of you are deeply involved in the world and
doing your best to make it a better place. But at least once a week
you're allowed to duck into this quiet, restful sanctuary, where
no one yells (not even you), where the flowers and the music are
both beautiful, and where you can count on there being a certain
order to things, setting you free to open your heart to the Divine
Presence that is sometimes hard to find outside.

Church is a reassuring place, in the midst of so much change.
These are the same boxed pews that people sat in when this nation

49

was still a teenager. This altar has been in the same place ever since. Many of the prayers we pray this morning are the same prayers that Christians have been praying for centuries, and the God to whom we pray has been the same God for a whole lot longer than that.

One of religion's central functions is to provide this kind of continuity to people whose lives are both fragile and short. Even if you make it to a hundred, you won't last as long as a nice chest of drawers or a good piece of crystal. Every time I use my Grandma Lucy's fancy etched wine glass, I cannot believe that she has been gone for almost fifty years now, while I am still holding that glass in my hand. Whose idea was that, for a glass to last longer than a grandma?

Maybe that's what we're *really* doing here this morning—hoping to deepen our ties to the *eternal* God, who can give fragile people like us something to hold on to when the headlines howl, the walls shake, and the earth moves underneath our feet.

I don't remember things being so bad fifty years ago, but I'm pretty sure that was because I was four. My father came through the Great Depression. My mother saved the tin foil off her gum wrappers during World War II. When I was six, my first-grade teacher taught us how to crawl under our desks in case of nuclear attack. That would have been the Bay of Pigs, right? Then there was the war in Vietnam and all those assassinations in the sixties, followed by a little giddy period of disco dancing and free love before the AIDS epidemic, the Gulf War, Rwanda, and 9/11.

These days I think it would be hard for even the most ardent optimist to argue with W. B. Yeats. "Things fall apart," he wrote in a poem called "The Second Coming," "the centre cannot hold";

> Mere anarchy is loosed upon the world,
> The blood-dimmed tide is loosed, and everywhere
> The ceremony of innocence is drowned;
> The best lack all conviction, while the worst
> Are full of passionate intensity.

Of course he wrote that in 1921, but my point is that if you came here this morning looking for some sanctuary from the world outside, then I'm afraid that today's not your day. It's

Apocalypse Now in the readings for this next-to-the-last Sunday of the church year, with Daniel on one side, predicting "'a time of anguish, such as has never occurred since nations first came into existence'" (12:1), and Jesus on the other, describing a doomsday full of sacrilege, suffering, and woe.

Episcopalians are usually protected from such things—protected not only by education and wealth but also by an unflappably sensible way of reading Scripture that causes us to ignore some of the more flamboyant parts. I'll bet most of you can count on one hand the number of sermons you have heard on the book of Revelation in an Episcopal church. Am I right? I'll bet your clergy have given you no help at all in identifying the antichrist, interpreting the mark of the beast, or figuring out whether the rapture will occur before, during, or after the great tribulation. True or false?

This semester I'm teaching a course in apocalyptic literature at Piedmont College—a subject I knew little about before offering the class. Fifteen students showed up, including several who have read the entire *Left Behind* series, and only one of whom is an unflappable Episcopalian. With two class sessions left to go, I would have to say that the biggest surprise has been my own naiveté about what a powerful hold the end time has on the popular imagination.

Once you start looking for it, it's *everywhere*—not only at the bookstore, the music store, on television, and at the movies but also—predictably, I suppose, given all those other venues—in American politics, where millions of voters are watching the Middle East for signs that the end-time alarm clock is about to ring. What's more, a significant number of those same people are willing to do whatever they can to help move the hands on that clock forward, even if they have to yank on them a little bit.

Unlike Jesus' disciples, who prompted his doomsday speech by asking him for signs of the end time, these people are pretty sure they already know what those signs are. They have studied the Scriptures. They have kept up with the headlines. They have done the math. While different groups of them have come up with significantly different answers, what they have in common is their dedication to being awake when the end time comes. They have no intention of being left behind, and they profess to know exactly what is required of anyone who wants to go with them to meet their Lord in the air.

This does not make them bad people, although their certainty about who is evil and who is good makes them pretty scary people, but in light of this morning's Gospel reading, I think they may have essentially misunderstood Jesus' message. Along the way, they may also be missing something essential about the nature of faith.

It's not hard to do. When you're listening to Jesus talk about the signs of the end time, it's easy to believe that he's offering you clues to a puzzle that you should be able to solve. Just figure out what the desolating sacrilege is and where it has been set up. Then figure out which mountains you're going to flee to. Then figure out how to tell the real Messiah from the false ones, and real prophets from imposters. Then dedicate yourself to staying awake until the alarm goes off, without getting distracted by all the mundane needs and griefs of everyday life.

That way maybe you can be excused before things fall apart. Or at the very least, maybe you can keep your grip when the blood-dimmed tide is loosed upon the world. Because you have paid attention, because you have done your homework, because you have stayed awake trimming your wick while more fragile people have fallen asleep all around you, maybe you can avoid getting sucked down the drain with them when the time comes. Because you have read the signs rightly, maybe you can hang on.

God knows I understand that wish. I even understand how it is possible to hear Jesus commending that very course of action. But when I listen again, I hear him saying something closer to the exact opposite, something more like this:

Give it up, everyone. I know you're scared, and when you get scared the first thing you want to do is run back to where you once felt safest. Go back to the church the way it was. Go back to the world the way it was. But there's no going back. When God's time comes, you won't have time to grab a coat. All those cans of beans you stored in the basement are going to rust right where they are. All that cash you stashed away is going to mildew. God will shorten the suffering, but the rest is out of your hands. So don't be led astray by people who pretend they know a secret way out. God's future is not a puzzle you can solve, any more than life's a game you can win by making all the right moves.

"But be alert." That's where Jesus stops this morning. "I have already told you everything."

It's tempting to think he means the part about the desolating sacrilege, along with the warning about the false prophets and messiahs, but that's hardly what you would call "everything." Even *he* doesn't seem to know when these things will come to pass. "Pray that it may not be in winter," he says. This leaves us with all the other things he has already told us, like the part about loving God with your whole heart, soul, and mind, and your neighbor as yourself. Or the part about being the salt of the earth. Or the part about giving to everyone who asks of you. Or the part about trusting God, though the waves threaten to swamp the boat.

That is just a fraction of what he has already told us, and it is plenty—plenty for now and plenty for any future of God's imagining, which in any case is entirely out of our hands. There will always be people who believe faith requires them to be certain about everything that God has in store, and to gain every advantage they can by figuring it all out ahead of time. Yet it seems entirely possible that faith is closer to the exact opposite—continuing to live the way we have been taught to live though we cannot be certain of anything, and entrusting the rest to God.

There will always be people who believe faith requires them to be certain about everything that God has in store, and to gain every advantage they can by figuring it all out ahead of time. Yet it seems entirely possible that faith is closer to the exact opposite.

If you think about it, the world has been ending for someone, somewhere, for as long as anyone can remember: Caesar, the Czar, the passenger pigeon, and the World Trade Towers have all gone down to the dust, taking whole eras with them—and still, two weeks from now, it will be Advent again, when even the headlines will soften a little bit at what is coming upon the world.

You remember how the Yeats poem ends:

> The darkness drops again; but now I know
> That twenty centuries of stony sleep
> Were vexed to nightmare by a rocking cradle,
> And what rough beast, its hour come round at last,
> Slouches towards Bethlehem to be born?

Let us pray: Eternal God, who commits to us the swift and solemn trust of life; since we do not know what a day may bring forth, but only that the hour for serving you is always present, may we wake to the instant claims of your holy will, not waiting for tomorrow, but yielding today.[1]

St. John's Church,
Lafayette Square, Washington, DC
Twenty-Fourth Sunday after Pentecost
November 19, 2006

Chapter Eight

Pre-Gaming the Apocalypse

Habakkuk 1:1–4; 2:1–4

> *"O LORD, how long shall I cry for help,*
> *and you will not listen?*
> *Or cry to you 'Violence!'*
> *and you will not save?"*
> —Habakkuk 1:2

Good morning, All Saints. I love this place so much. It doesn't seem to matter whether I get back here once every couple of years or once every couple of decades: this is my home church, which makes you my church family and me your odd Aunt Barbara, whether we have ever met or not. Like you, I keep coming back here because it is the place I feel most sane, most accompanied, most drawn out of myself to be with people whose lives may be as different from mine as they can be, but whose hearts I trust beyond all reason.

Maybe it's because we're all on our best behavior here, or maybe it's because the windows let us drop the curtains on what's outside them for a while. Maybe it's the compounding interest on all the beauty that has been deposited in us through the years here, or maybe it's the promises we keep making together: to seek and serve Christ in all persons, to love our neighbors as ourselves, to strive for justice and peace among all people, to respect the dignity of every human being. *All persons. All people. Every human being.* That's a lot to promise. *I will, with God's help.*

You can't say things like that more than once or twice without feeling close to the people who are saying them with you, even if you don't know their names or zip codes—maybe even *because* you don't know their names or zip codes, any more than they know yours. A certain level of anonymity can be a great aid to feeling warmly toward other people. A certain distance can permit a broader embrace.

This may not be something a preacher ought to say,
but I have always found it easier to love humanity as a
whole than to love any particular human being
for more than an hour or two at a time.

This may not be something a preacher ought to say, but I have always found it easier to love humanity as a whole than to love any particular human being for more than an hour or two at a time. It helps to imagine them naked. I learned that from a training manual for flight attendants. The rest of the time I pray to God to remind me that I can be as hard to love as anyone God ever met—and if that were not true of me as well as a large percentage of God's beloved children, then Jesus would not have had very much to say or do while he was here. Love is *hard*. Justice and peace cost more than most of us have budgeted for them. Respecting the dignity of every human being? *I will, with God's help.* Just please don't tell me how they vote.

Nine days from now we will have a new president. According to sources as varied as *The Wall Street Journal, salon.com,* and the American Psychological Association, record numbers of us are suffering from what some mental health professionals are calling Pre-Election Stress Disorder, and others (who suspect that the condition may last a while longer) are calling Political Anxiety Disorder. It affects millennials at almost the same rate as people in their seventies. It troubles people of all colors from both parties.

Even if you have been spared, you may recognize some of the more common symptoms in your family and friends: irritability, sleeplessness, weight gain, increased alcohol consumption, feelings of powerlessness or resentment, avoidance of conversations involving politics, more conflict at home, less productivity at work, persistent low-grade anger, and something called "cognitive dissonance," which is the crunching sound your brain makes when it hits new information that contradicts what you thought you knew about the world.

Your next-door neighbors hammer a sign into their front yard that tells you they aren't who you thought they were. The large crowds at the other candidate's rallies suggest that your values aren't as mainstream as you believed they were. Some of your Facebook friends post things that make you want to get up and make sure your doors are locked. As David Brooks wrote in his op-ed piece this week, "Anxiety is coursing through American society. It has become its own destructive character on the national stage."[1] Bizarrely, that makes it the one thing voters can agree on at the moment: left or right, red or blue, him or her, we all agree that if the other team wins, the end is near.

Why am I talking about this in church? Because I think it's a spiritual problem. Because I think our corporate stress around this election crashes right into the promises we make every time we baptize someone into the body of Christ. Because Habakkuk showed up in the readings for today—the only time he ever shows up in the readings on a Sunday—which means that today is his only chance to be heard for three more years, and he is the perfect prophet for anyone suffering from Political Anxiety Disorder.

> O LORD, how long shall I cry for help,
>   and you will not listen?
> Or cry to you, "Violence!"
>   and you will not save?
> Why do you make me see wrongdoing
>   and look at trouble?
> Destruction and violence are before me;
>   strife and contention arise.
> So the law becomes slack
>   and justice never prevails.
> The wicked surround the righteous—
>   therefore judgment comes forth perverted. (vv. 2–4)

No one knows anything about Habakkuk except what is in his book. The political enemies on his horizon are the Chaldeans, a "fierce and impetuous nation" whose "horses are swifter than leopards, more menacing than wolves at dusk." They seize dwellings not their own. They gather captives like sand. Apocalypse is right around the corner. But Habakkuk's argument is not with them. His argument is with God. Why is God letting the bad guys win? What has happened to the God of justice? Habakkuk thought he knew who God was, but the Chaldean menace is messing with his head. The Divine Listener will not listen. The Divine Savior will not save. Meet cognitive dissonance, circa 600 BCE.

Against all odds, Habakkuk decides to remain faithful even if God won't. He stations himself on the rampart of his fortress and waits for God to answer his complaint. *How long?* That's what he wants to know, but there are no term limits in his day. He might wait nine days and he might wait eight years.

When God finally answers him, the news is not good.

The Chaldeans are serving a purpose, God tells Habakkuk. Their arrogance will circle back on them, but that is not your business. Your business is to write the vision—to write it so plainly that even those who hurry by can read it. "For there is still a vision for the appointed time," God says to Habakkuk; "it speaks of the end, and does not lie." If it seems slow; wait for it. It is on its way; it will arrive right on time (2:3).

But what about the meantime (the *very* mean time)? The spirit of the proud "is not right in them," God says, "but the righteous live by their faith" (v. 4).

Lots of people think Paul said that, since it shows up more than once in his letters, but Habakkuk said it first. Every three years he gets to say it right here in church, reminding us that before Jesus and after Jesus, God's people have always lived by faith— by continuing to do what they know is right, regardless of what the leopards and wolves are doing. At the same time, Habakkuk reminds us that the faithful do not cease to be faithful when they call God to account. Job did it. Jeremiah did it. Depending on how you read Jesus' last words from the cross, he did it too.

The fact that these laments have ended up in Scripture tells us there is something sacred about them, something we need not fear doing ourselves. Perhaps it helps God to hear the faithful cry out while the Chaldeans are serving their painful purpose? In his bestselling book *Between the World and Me*, Ta-Nehisi Coates says, "History is not solely in our hands. And still you are called to struggle, not because it assures you victory but because it assures you an honorable and sane life."[2]

That is far more eloquent than the advice therapists across the country are giving patients with Political Anxiety Disorder right now. "Get more exercise." That shows up on a lot of lists. So does "limit social media," "stick with facts," and "watch *Saturday Night Live*." One therapist suggested making a list of things you do now that you will still be able to do regardless of who is elected. Another recommended finding something practical to do right now: call and encourage a voter in a swing state, offer a ride to someone you know is reluctant to drive. Action is key, no matter how limited the outcome.

No one said, "Have faith," which didn't surprise me since I was reading *HuffPost* and not *Christianity Today*, but God didn't say anything to Habakkuk about *having* faith. God talked about *living by* faith—a small but vital difference that removes faith from anyone's possession and gives it back again as a way of life.

I heard something close to that in the advice of a counselor who practices in suburban DC. When couples come to him for help with election anxiety, he says, he reminds them to stop downloading negativity from their environment and "focus on the kind of partners and parents they most want to be and let their deeper values guide them."

"Just do something selfless to help someone else and you'll feel much better," he said. "You've got to serve other people to be happy."[3]

That was in the *Washington Post*, not the Gospel reading for today, but I think it still works. Does your Political Anxiety Disorder have you up a tree? Are you hoping to see the Savior without bumping up against that tall crowd of rowdy people who keep

getting in your way? Good luck with that. Better hope you see
the Savior before he sees you, because when he does he's going to
tell you to come down from your watch post and do something
selfless for someone else—like sit down to supper with a bunch
of people whose names you don't even know. Some of them will
be as anxious about eating with you as you are about eating with
them. Some of them will be voting the other way. *C'est la vie.*
How else are you going to let your deeper values guide you into
a life worth living? How else are you going to keep the promises
you have made? *All persons. All people. Every human being.*

It's the vision God has given us. It's what we're here to practice.
It's what keeps us coming back. So we will, with God's help—for
nine more days, and all the days to come.

All Saints' Episcopal Church,
Atlanta, Georgia
October 30, 2016*

---

*Nine days later, Donald Trump was elected the 45th president of the United
States.

Chapter Nine

How to Lose Your Life Every Day

Romans 12:9–21

Bless those who persecute you; bless and do not curse them. Rejoice with those who rejoice, weep with those who weep. Live in harmony with one another; do not be haughty, but associate with the lowly; do not claim to be wiser than you are. Do not repay anyone evil for evil, but take thought for what is noble in the sight of all. If it is possible, so far as it depends on you, live peaceably with all.
—Romans 12:14–18

Let me begin by saying how happy I am to be among Baptists this morning. When the new semester begins at Piedmont College, I always do a quick hand check to see what kind of help I am going to get teaching my classes. I count on the Catholics to know how worship works. They may only go to mass when they are home for the holidays, but when we get around to discussing why Catholics have seven sacraments and Protestants only have two, they can usually give textbook definitions of all seven that they learned in first grade.

The Presbyterians are the orderly thinkers, unafraid of long words such as predestination. The Methodists have a sweet spot for social service. The Lutherans know where their name came from and understand what the Reformation was all about. There are never any Episcopalians in class, but if there were, I would count on them to help explain why common prayer is more important to us than common beliefs.

These days there are plenty of students who do not identify with any mainline denomination, but the majority of those who do are Baptists. I count on them to take the Bible seriously, and to know that Jonah was not one of the twelve disciples. Last Thursday I was talking to a full room about how the Bible was both a book and a library full of books bound together for the first time in the fourth century.

"How many of you can name all sixty-six books in order?" I asked. About eight students raised their hands. "And how many of you are Baptists?" I asked. All of the hands stayed up, including one that belonged to a serious-looking girl in the front. Her hand was only halfway up, though, like she was hoping I wouldn't see.

"Take it away," I said to her, and she looked like she had just been arrested.

"Not *here*," she pleaded. I leaned down so only she could hear me. "Just the first five? Please?"

"Genesis, Exodus, Leviticus, Numbers, Deuteronomy," she said, dropping her eyes at the end. Then I went on with my lecture, but it was clear she couldn't stop. Her lips kept moving for about the next forty-five seconds. Then she sighed (Revelation!) and sat up straight again, while somewhere in the world a Sunday school teacher remembered that girl's face without the slightest idea why.

So I'm counting on you here—not to follow her act, but to hang with me through a close reading of Romans—because if you know your Bibles, you also know that Paul's teaching is not as straightforward as it is sometimes made out to be.

Yes, he is the apostle who says that those who trust God are excused from following the law as the road to salvation. Faith in God is all that is required, Paul says, for "'everyone who calls on the name of the Lord shall be saved'" (Rom. 10:13). All you have to do is believe that you are saved and you are. Nothing else is required.

Does that sound familiar to you? It sounds familiar to me.

But here's the complication: the same Paul who said we could stop worrying about the requirements of the law turned right around and gave us a whole new list of imperatives.

Let love be genuine.
Hate what is evil.
Hold fast to what is good.
Love one another with mutual affection.
Outdo one another in showing honor.
Do not lag in zeal.
Be ardent in spirit.
Serve the Lord.
Rejoice in hope.
Be patient in suffering.
Persevere in prayer.
Contribute to the needs of the saints.
Extend hospitality to strangers.
Bless those who persecute you.
Bless and do not curse them.
Rejoice with those who rejoice.
Weep with those who weep.
Live in harmony with one another.
Do not be haughty.
But associate with the lowly.
Do not claim to be wiser than you are.
Do not repay anyone evil for evil.
But take thought for what is noble in the sight of all.
If it is possible, so far as it depends on you, live peaceably
    with all.
Beloved, never avenge yourselves.
But leave room for the wrath of God.
If your enemies are hungry, feed them.
If they are thirsty, give them something to drink.
Do not be overcome by evil.
But overcome evil with good.

All told, that's thirteen verses from Romans 12 with thirty new rules for Christian life in them. Could I please just have the Ten Commandments back?

Of course, Paul never says that salvation depends on following the imperatives on his list. Track back to the beginning of the chapter and you get the context: this is Paul's appeal to people who *already* belong to God, who are *already* committed to worshiping God. It's not a before-you-pass-go list; it's an after-you-land-on-home list. So that offers some relief. But it also kicks things up a notch, because if this is a list of what it means to worship God—to be truly and recognizably Christian—then some of us are, well—how shall I put it?—*not.*

If this is a list of what it means to worship God—to be truly and recognizably Christian—then some of us are, well—how shall I put it?—*not.*

Some of us might be, if what we are doing together right now were the only kind of worship Paul was talking about—the kind that starts at 11:00 and ends at noon, so that you know when you're on the clock and when you're off. You look like people with whom I could live in harmony for at least the next hour. I think I could hold off avenging myself until after lunch—especially with your pastor and the deacons here keeping an eye on things, reminding us to extend hospitality to the visitors and to put something in the plate for the needs of the saints. I'm feeling pretty ardent in the spirit—aren't you? I'm feeling like holding fast to what is good. *Let us serve the Lord!*

Apparently Paul had something more extensive in mind—this kind of worship, sure, but also the kind you offer every minute of every day, with whoever happens to be standing right in front of you, whether you feel like it or not, with no one to remind you what to do next or why it is important—the kind of worship you engage in all the time without benefit of clergy, sanctuary, congregation, or closing hymn. All Paul lets us have is an order of service—the one I just read—which doesn't tell us *what* to do or *when*, exactly, but which does give us *something* to do no matter where we are on this earth or whom we are with.

Half-listening to your mother on the telephone while you check your email with your free hand?

"Let love be genuine."

Trying to beat the old guy with the raggedy package in his arms through the door of the post office because you have a much smaller package and your lunch hour is almost up?

"Outdo one another in showing honor."

Sitting in a meeting with someone who points out the flaws in everything you say?

"Bless those who persecute you."

Putting off calling a friend who has just been fired for the second time in a year because you don't know what to say?

"Weep with those who weep."

This is such quiet, unsung, under-the-radar worship that it's not enough for a lot of Christians I know—the new ones, especially—who want to stand up in front of microphones and give their testimonies to thousands of people (there's nothing wrong with that) or rebuild a church in Haiti and fill it with the finest furnishings anyone in that part of the world has ever seen (there may be nothing wrong with that either).

Depending on where you are in your life of faith—and maybe on your temperament, too—doing something big can seem like the best way to serve God. Let other people see it, make sure they know you're doing it because you're Christian, and hope that something in their lives changes as a result. Then go home feeling good about yourself, because you have done a good thing. In your own way, with the resources available to you, you have taken up your cross and followed Jesus. You have held it up high so everyone can see—so they can make no mistake about whom you worship—and you have left the rest to God.

Matthew would love that. "'If any want to become my followers,'" he quotes Jesus as saying, "'let them deny themselves and take up their cross and follow me'" (16:24). But Paul's order of service does not say a single thing about taking up a cross. I even checked his other letters to be sure. He talks about the cross of Christ, but never as something we're supposed to pick up.

Unlike Matthew, Paul seems less interested in the big, once-and-for-all kind of sacrifice than he is in the living, every-single-day kind—so *not* big, so easy to miss, that a nursing mother can pull it off, or a teen who sits at the wrong table in the lunchroom *on purpose*, or a guy who stops for coffee on his way to work and orders a double latte for his office rival. You can correct me on this, but I think if he handed it over and said, "I'm only doing this because I'm Christian," that would cancel the whole thing out.

"Let love be genuine," Paul says. That's the sacrifice he's interested in—the kind that doesn't necessarily make you feel *better about yourself* but is almost guaranteed to make you think *less about yourself* as you keep working the order of service. It's hard to focus on your own spiritual accomplishments while you are rejoicing with those who rejoice and weeping with those who weep. It's hard to count the points you are collecting for being Christian while you're fixing something for your enemies to eat or pouring them a glass of sweet tea.

I don't think Paul would *object* if you decided to take up your cross and find some way to lose your life that made headline news, but it would be just like him to ask how much ego you had wrapped up in that, how much you were counting on getting out of your striking display of Christian faith.

"Do not be haughty."

"Do not claim to be wiser than you are."

Paul seems more interested in all the ways you can lose your life every day by making love genuine—whether anyone notices or not, whether it makes you feel good about yourself or not—just sizing up whatever situation you happen to be in, pausing long enough to weigh the choices before you, and choosing the one that you think will make love most real, even if it costs you something.

It's not like it *has* to cost you something or it doesn't count. Some of the things on Paul's list sound really satisfying—like loving one another with mutual affection and outdoing one another in showing honor. Those both sound like win-win propositions to me. But being patient in suffering? Not so much. Blessing those who persecute me? I have some real questions about that one. May I perform the blessing privately, or do I have to do it where my persecutor can hear me? I could probably do it face-to-face if I had to, but it would have to be really quick and formal. *God bless you for your inexplicable hostility toward me, and by God's grace may these words land like burning coals on your head. Amen.*

That sounds satisfying for all the wrong reasons, but doing it with genuine love, like Paul says? I would have to give up so much to get anywhere near that. I would have to give up being genuinely wounded, genuinely right, genuinely mad. That doesn't sound satisfying at all.

Then there's that imperative about living in harmony with one another—proof that Paul was never married, had children, or stayed in one congregation very long. I still remember the day I was in the checkout line at the grocery store when the young man scanning my purchases looked up at me and said, "They say marriage is all about compromise. Is that true?"

I could not figure out why he asked me that. Was it something I bought? Did I remind him of someone? Was he thinking of proposing to someone?

"Yes," I said, "it's true."

"I was afraid you were going to say that," he said.

Living in any kind of harmony with other people means giving up some of what you want so that they can have some of what they want—and not just groceries, either. You may also be called upon to give up some of what you want in terms of how you will spend your money, how you will organize your time, how you will keep your living space, and whom you will invite into it.

If you belong to this church or any other one, then you can probably think of some other things that go on the list of "what I have given up for harmony." But did you give them up with genuine love? That's what Paul wants to know. If you gave them up because you got outvoted, or worn down, or because you have never been any good at standing up for what you want, then "living in harmony" may still be on your to-do list—a part of your daily worship that you can count on getting lots of opportunities to practice.

Thank goodness that is what we call it—practicing faith—which is not the same thing as earning salvation or winning God's love. If Paul's list gets harder as it goes on, "do not lag in zeal! Be ardent in spirit!" This is how the slow love of God works on those who *already* belong to God, who are *already* committed to living the kinds of lives that take lots and lots of practice, which is why there is only enough time for us to get started during our hour here this morning.

Yet starting here is how we remember that worship is something people do with other people—that being truly and recognizably Christian has always had more to do with how we live together than with how brightly we shine alone—and that in any case there is only so much that any one of us can do. The ego may not know that, but love does. Love knows that the kind of power it has is not the power to command.

"If it is possible, so far as it depends on you, live peaceably with all." Paul knows it may not always be possible, because everything does not depend on you, but even when you're not getting any cooperation, you still have a few strong moves left.

> Beloved, never avenge yourselves;
> But leave room for the wrath of God.
> "If your enemies are hungry, feed them;
> If they are thirsty, give them something to drink."
> Do not be overcome by evil,
> But overcome evil with good.

If these are Paul's commandments, they embody his Golden Rule: *Love as you are beloved. Do unto others as God has done unto you.* He never says it outright like that, but the implication is clear.

The only reason we have the slightest idea what genuine love looks like is because we have been loved that way, by God and by one another. That's what saves us over and over, so that there are all sorts of things we never have to do again.

We don't have to avenge ourselves. We don't have to take matters into our own hands. We don't have to get even. We don't have to punish our enemies. We don't have to appear wiser than we are. We don't have to shield ourselves from joy or sorrow. We don't have to fear strangers. We don't have to lock our hearts.

Above all, we don't have to do anything to be Beloved. That's a given. Everything else comes *after*.

Millbrook Baptist Church,
Raleigh, North Carolina
Eleventh Sunday after Pentecost
August 28, 2011

Chapter Ten

Sabbath Rest

Isaiah 58:6–9

Is not this the fast that I choose:
to loose the bonds of injustice,
to undo the thongs of the yoke,
to let the oppressed go free,
and to break every yoke?
—Isaiah 58:6

Good evening. My name is Barbara and I will be your server tonight. I have five courses to set before you. Your bill has been paid in full, including my gratuity. I hope you enjoy your meal.

The Amuse-Bouche (The Mouth Pleaser)

Taste and see that God is good.
Taste and see that the earth is lush.
Taste and see that those who laid this feast before us know their Scriptures well. There is no penny pinching here, no calorie counting, no hygienic balancing of the four food groups. There are times for all of those things, but tonight is not one of them. Tonight the Communion Table is overflowing with grapes, hummus, cheese, bread—truly, a feast of fat things, of well-aged wines strained clear.

Tonight we are invited to God's Table, where there is always plenty, whether it looks like a huge loaf of challah or a saltine cracker, broken into as many pieces as there are people to be fed.

Tonight we can give up pretending that our bodies and souls sleep in separate bedrooms, with one full of creature comforts and the other as bare as a nun's cell. The host of this feast knows that we come whole to God's Table, where every kind of human hunger is fed. Body and soul both sigh with pleasure here, falling back in love again. So taste and see that God is good. Your tongue knows this, as surely as the Holy Spirit within you. If your mouth is pleased, the pleasure is all God's.

The Starter

All over the world this Friday night, our mothers and fathers in faith are welcoming the Queen of the Sabbath. They have been doing this for thousands of years—before there was a Torah, an Israel, or a Church. Most will tell you that the Queen has saved their lives. Without her, they could never have survived Pharaoh, Nebuchadnezzar, or Caesar. Without her, they could never have survived their own ambition, genius, or restlessness. If they had not stopped to welcome her every seventh day, laying aside everything else upon which their lives depended, there is no telling what might have happened to them. They might have worked themselves to death. They might have served other gods. They might have forgotten who they were.

If you have ever been to a Shabbat service, then you remember that moment when everyone stands and turns toward the door, waiting for God's own Friday-night bride to arrive. She never lets them down. Every seventh day, she appears when evening falls, trailing peace behind her like a train of fragrant flowers. *Shabbat shalom!* That's what the congregation murmurs, every single time. Has she ever been more beautiful? Have they ever needed to see her more?

Once the Queen arrives, it doesn't matter if your work is done. It doesn't matter whether you got finished with the shopping, the planning, the fixing, the pleasing. It doesn't even matter whether you finished making the world a better place, because once God's bride arrives, the wedding party has begun. It is time to boogie. Pass the grapes, please. No, not those little green ones—the big purple ones, fat as plums.

The Fish Course

Watch out for the bones. Unlike the Protestants among us, our mothers and fathers in faith see a direct link between how they respond to God and how God responds to them. Call it "works-righteousness" if you must, but the language of exchange is right there in the book of Isaiah.

> If you remove the yoke from among you,
>   the pointing of the finger, the speaking of evil,
> if you offer your food to the hungry
>   and satisfy the needs of the afflicted,
> then your light shall rise in the darkness
>   and your gloom be like the noonday.
> The Lord will guide you continually,
>   and satisfy your needs in parched places,
>   and make your bones strong;
> and you shall be like a watered garden,
>   like a spring of water,
>   whose waters never fail.
>
> *(vv. 9b–11)*

The prophet is not threatening anyone. He is offering helpful information about how the world really works. It is not possible for our light to rise in the darkness while there is still the pointing of the finger, the speaking of evil among us. Even God cannot lift our gloom while we persist in keeping the hungry away from our food or working harder to satisfy our own needs than the needs of the afflicted.

But there is another way, which does not separate our health from the health of our neighbors, who hunger for justice as much as bread. Freeing them, we are freed. Feeding them, we are fed.

When we get it deep down in our bones that there is only one feast, set for all God's people, we will haul all our best dishes out of the church and set them before the world.

> Then you shall call, and the LORD will answer;
> you shall cry for help, and he will say, Here I am.

> *(v. 9a)*

The Meat Course

I wish we read whole chapters of Scripture in church—with no ellipses, skipped verses, or well-intentioned censoring of things that might scare the children or cause a visitor to ask, "What is *that* doing in a holy book?" In the case of tonight's reading from Isaiah, there are a lot more conditional clauses that follow the ones we just heard.

> If you refrain from trampling the sabbath,
> from pursuing your own interests on my holy day;
> if you call the sabbath a delight
> and the holy day of the LORD honorable;
> if you honor it, not going your own ways,
> serving your own interests, or pursuing your own affairs;
> then you shall take delight in the LORD,
> and I will make you ride upon the heights of the earth;
> I will feed you with the heritage of your ancestor Jacob,
> for the mouth of the LORD has spoken.

> *(vv. 13–14)*

Here is more helpful information about how things really work. No one can break yokes nonstop. No one can satisfy the needs of the afflicted 24/7. According to Isaiah, it is as sacred to rest one day a week as it is to loose the bonds of injustice the other six. Honoring the Sabbath is as vital to our health as offering food to the hungry. Small wonder, then, that some of us are ailing, both in our bodies and in the bodies of our congregations.

When did we decide to let the market keep time for us instead of God? With what sick logic did we decide that the world's drumbeat of drivenness and collapse promised us more than God's rhythm of hard work and reliable rest? Refraining from work one day a week is not good advice. It is divine command, as vital to the survival of God's people as refraining from idolatry or murder.

That resting one whole day every week should seem impossible to so many of us is a sign that we have taken a wrong turn somewhere. What bridegroom told us we could leave the Sabbath bride at the altar? What god taught us that rest is a sign of weakness or sloth? Is it because Jesus never rested? "The Sabbath was made for humankind," he said, "and not humankind for the Sabbath" (Mark 2:27). But does that erase the Sabbath or does it fortify its importance?

Anyone with no time for a wedding clearly has too much to do.

The Palate Cleanser

As Anne Lamott wrote in one of her books, we are not punished *for* our sins; we are punished *by* them.[1] Please note that there is no punishment in Isaiah's prophecy. There are only rewards—strong bones, light and delight, continual guidance, satisfied needs—all those good gifts left unwrapped on the altar by those who went their own ways, pursuing their own interests on God's holy day.

The Salad Course

According to the rabbis, those who keep the Sabbath keep all the other commandments rolled up in that one. One day a week, they live as if all their work were done. One day a week, they receive life as God's free gift at zero percent interest with no money down. One day a week, they pull the plug on all other gods.

Doing so, they engage the single most countercultural practice of faith, upon which their lives depend. Keeping Sabbath is how they survive civilization. It is how they beat amnesia. It is how they remember the one God's true name.

Last week someone gave me a cartoon from the *New Yorker* that is going into my Sabbath file. It shows God standing on a bank of clouds with the earth way off in the sky. The earth is much smaller, in fact, than the gas grill in front of which God is standing, spatula in hand, with a can of beer on the cutting board. "On the Seventh Day," the caption reads.

I have an alternative caption from the Jerusalem Talmud: "You will be held accountable for permissible pleasures needlessly denied."[2] I wish Jesus had said that in the Sermon on the Mount somewhere, to remind us that pleasure is part of God's will for our lives. To deny it for no good reason—to turn down God's burger in order to go mow the lawn—is a serious case of misplaced loyalty. Even John Calvin bowled on Sundays.[3]

The Dessert Course, at Last

Jesus said, "'The kingdom of God is as if someone would scatter seed on the ground, and would sleep and rise night and day, and the seed would sprout and grow, he does not know how'" (Mark 4:26–27). *Naaah.* That can't be right. Dedicated farmers are essential to seeds sprouting and growing. Seeds that grow by themselves are called "weeds."

If Jesus was really looking for people to help him spread the gospel, he should have said, "The kingdom of God is as if someone would plow a field, fertilize it, plant seeds six inches apart in straight rows, hold umbrellas over them when it rained hard to keep them from washing away, haul buckets from the creek to water them when they were dry, wave birds and insects away during the day, and sleep fitfully at night for fear of what might be eating the tender plants in the dark. Then he would get up early the next morning and start the whole routine all over again, knowing the seeds did not stand a chance without him."

The health of our Sabbath practice has everything to do with the health of our trust in God's abundance. Those who walk away from their fields one day a week have faith that the fields will be there when they return.

The health of our Sabbath practice has everything to do with the health of our trust in God's abundance. Those who walk away from their fields one day a week have faith that the fields will be there when they return. They may even have come to expect that some things will have grown without their help, while others died in spite of their care. They are able to rest because they have surrendered the illusion that their work makes life happen. They have faith that God alone gives the growth.

If we trusted that, what else might we do with our time?

The seed is in the ground, friends. You have been putting it there all week. Now sit down, for God's sake, and let it grow. There's not another thing for you to do, because there is a Lord of the Sabbath and it's not you. So welcome to the wedding banquet, where gifts of light and delight for your body and soul have been waiting for you to open them forever.

Taste and see that God is good; and how happy are those who take refuge here.

Washington National Cathedral,[*]
Washington, DC
May 10, 2007

---

[*]At a Friday-night celebration of Holy Eucharist, in front of an altar heaped with grapes, hummus, cheese, bread, and flanked with two full cases of wine.

Chapter Eleven

Divine Forgetfulness

Deuteronomy 24:10–22; Acts 28:1–16

When you reap your harvest in your field and forget a sheaf in the field, you shall not go back to get it; it shall be left for the alien, the orphan, and the widow, so that the LORD your God may bless you in all your undertakings.

—Deuteronomy 24:19

The two lessons set before us this evening open two very different doors on faith. In the passage from Acts, the apostle Paul— shipwrecked on Malta—shakes a poisonous snake from his hand as if it were a midge, cures a man by laying hands on his head, then heals everyone on the island who is suffering from any kind of disease. These miracles bring him both honor and reward. When Paul and his companions set sail, their ship has been fully stocked by grateful islanders. They have *more*, not *less*, than they did when they arrived.

Based on the mail I receive from spiritual seekers, this is the kind of faith most people are looking for. They want the kind that will grant them immunity from death and danger, the kind that will give them power to do things ordinary people cannot do. If they just had this, they say, they would have all the proof they need: that God really does exist, that God really is powerful, that

God really does give power to those who believe. Call it the kind of faith that moves mountains.

The passage from Deuteronomy has no miracles in it. It focuses on the kind of faith that moves *us* instead—to respect the dignity of debtors, to pay laborers the same day they work, to leave wheat in the field for those who cannot afford to buy it at market. None of these acts of faith are going to make headlines like shaking a snake from your hand. Our only satisfaction will be knowing that we have kept faith with one of God's commands, which has made us slightly more generous than we might otherwise have been, though in profoundly ordinary ways.

There are nine commands in this short section of Torah. With the exception of the one about parents and children not being put to death for each other's sins, the commands are all about how those at the top of the food chain are to treat those at the bottom.

According to those who know, there once was a time when such commands weren't necessary for God's people—back when kinship bonds were strong and extended families caught those whose safety nets had broken. But success changed things. People moved into big urban areas where some of them made a lot more money than others. It was no longer possible to know all of the neighbors, some of whom only showed up when they were raising money for something—their own rent, for all you knew. You could often tell the renters from the owners by how badly their places needed a paint job, but you knew it wasn't their fault. It was the landlord's fault, and still the kids were being treated badly at school because they walked home to such shabby houses.

You get the picture. Things haven't changed all that much in 2,500 years. "You shall love your neighbor as yourself"—that's in Torah too (Lev. 19:18). But remind me, please: who is my neighbor?

In these verses from Deuteronomy, the neighbor is anyone to whom you are economically related. Your neighbor is anyone to whom you lend something or from whom you borrow it; anyone who works for you or for whom you work; anyone who sells something you need to live or who buys or barters it from you. As much as we like to think it's compassion that makes us kin, it's not. It's economics: the daily give and take of the goods and services that make life possible both for those who have and those who have not.

Is there an app that allows you to track the progress of a five-pound note through the system? If not, I hope you will invent one—so you can see how the note you use to buy bread goes into the bank to pay the clerk who sold it to you, who spends it on petrol for his car, so that it becomes the property of the oil company that is still paying to clean up the spill where the fish you ate on Friday night was once caught and may be again. But don't get distracted by the fish! Keep your eye on the five-pound note, which has now gone into the pocket of one of the out-of-work fishermen as part of the company's reparation to the local community, who will use it to buy bread to pay the clerk who spends it on petrol for *her* car.

Of course, there was no paper money when Deuteronomy was written. It was more often *stuff* that changed hands: grinding stones, garments, olive oil, cooking pots. You can tell that from the first command, which says that when you make someone a loan and ask for collateral, you may not go into that person's house and take it. You must wait outside for the person to bring it out to you. This isn't a command about meeting the requirements of the law, in other words. It's a command about preserving the dignity of those who must ask for others' help.

If you accept someone's cloak as collateral, the next command says, and the person is so poor that the cloak doubles as a bed blanket, you may not sleep in it yourself. You must return it every evening by sunset so that the person may sleep in it and bless you. Presumably this means going back every morning to get the cloak back ("Umm, I'm here to take your blanket again"), which sounds like a very effective way to shame a lender ("Look, why don't you just keep the blanket and we'll shake hands on the loan instead?").

These are *very unusual* commands, not least because they place limits on the *rich*. When you hire day laborers, the next command says, make sure you pay them before the sun goes down. It may not be a big deal for you to wait three days for a check to clear, but your workers have kids at home waiting for them to come through the door with a grocery sack. Your workers shouldn't have to explain that to you, either. They worked today, so you pay them today. Whether they are brand-new immigrants or third-generation locals, getting their wages from you should not cost them one cent of dignity.

As a Christian, I'm used to thinking of these commands in terms of charity, but the next three of them kick that notion up a notch. When you leave a sheaf of wheat in the field, or when you beat your olive trees, or when you gather the grapes of your vineyard, says the Lord, don't go back to make sure you get every last one that belongs to you. Leave some for those who don't have land to grow things on. Leave some for those with no alpha males to look out for them.

But why just *leave* something for them, a charitable person might ask? Why not go the whole distance and gather the food, wash it, bag and deliver it to the poor people's doorsteps? Wouldn't that be the kinder thing to do?

Perhaps. But if you have ever been on the receiving end of such charity, you know that the hand that gives is always higher than the hand that receives. Think about it. Would you rather answer the door to find a group of good people bearing gifts for your needy family (with their own need for you to praise their goodness all over their faces), or would you rather know the fields where you are welcome to go at the end of the day with your *own* baskets to gather your *own* food for your *own* family, so that they rejoice to see *you* coming through the door instead of some well-meaning strangers?

This is the point at which it becomes clear that these commands are not about exercising *charity*. They are about exercising *divine justice*, as God requires those who have a lot to leave some for those who have little, without standing around to be seen or thanked.

The most puzzling command in the whole list—the one that has kept the rabbis busy—is the one about the sheaf left in the field. Did you hear the key verb when it went by? "When you reap your harvest in your field and *forget* a sheaf in the field, you shall not go back to get it; it shall be left for the alien, the orphan, and the widow, so that the LORD your God may bless you in all your undertakings" (emphasis added).

Come again? When you reap your harvest and *forget* a sheaf? This is very odd. How do you fulfill a command by forgetting something instead of remembering it? Can a deed really be called good if you didn't do it on purpose? But that's what the commandment says: when you remember that you forgot the sheaf, don't do anything about it. Just leave it for the people who will come for it later. But remember that you can't *leave* it for them in the first place. You have to have *forgotten* it first.

This may be the most charming commandment in the book— especially for people my age, who are always forgetting everything—but it is clearly not about cultivating memory loss as a spiritual practice. Instead, I think, it is about becoming the kind of person who isn't counting sheaves all the time. It is about becoming the kind of person who no longer worries about getting every olive off every tree and every grape off every vine—because there is plenty, really—plenty and some to spare—not only for you, the alien, the widow, and the orphan, but also for the deer, the rabbit, and the raven, who are members of the community as well.

Not many of us have wheat fields or vineyards anymore. Some of us don't even have olive trees in clay pots, but I'll bet you don't need my help to bring this teaching up to date. What would it take for you to be free enough to forget to gather up every bit of what is yours? How secure would you have to be, to skip getting down on your knees every day to make sure you didn't miss a single olive or grape?

What would it take for you to be free enough to forget to gather up every bit of what is yours? How secure would you have to be, to skip getting down on your knees every day to make sure you didn't miss a single olive or grape?

As I said at the start, this is a long way from the kind of faith that wants to move mountains—the kind that longs for more miracles, more power, a more direct line to God. There's nothing wrong with any of that, I suppose, except that so few people seem satisfied by the amount of power they get, whereas anyone, absolutely anyone, can have faith enough to be moved by God's justice, especially when it's as simple as making a micro-loan with no collateral, or paying a laborer's wages on time, or leaving a whole row of snow peas in the garden with a sign that says, "Help Yourself—Yes, You."

Who knows? You might even forget a couple of five-pound notes on the dresser the next time you stay in a hotel room and not go back to get them. They shall be left for the housekeeper, so that the Lord your God may bless you in all your undertakings.

It's up to us, really. But if we choose the commands instead of the miracles, then when our ships sail we will have *less*, not *more*, than we did when we arrived—less stuff, less guilt, less stress—and maybe a little more bliss as well, thanks to our *divine forgetfulness*, and the good Lord who showed us the way.

Evensong at Winchester Cathedral,
United Kingdom
July 5, 2015

Chapter Twelve

The Good Heretic

Luke 10:25–37

"But a Samaritan while traveling came near him; and when he saw him, he was moved with pity. He went to him and bandaged his wounds, having poured oil and wine on them. Then he put him on his own animal, brought him to an inn, and took care of him. The next day he took out two denarii, gave them to the innkeeper, and said, 'Take care of him; and when I come back, I will repay you whatever more you spend.'"

—Luke 10:33–35

One of the things I love most about the Bible is the security leaks in it. All the best sacred texts have them. There you are, feeling safe within the covers of your sacred book, counting on it to support your sense of having made the right choices where God is concerned, and all of a sudden the book lets a heretic in— someone who does not think like you think, or act like you act— someone who has clearly made the wrong choices where God is concerned, and yet your sacred text honors that person, making him or her the hero of the story, while you stand on the sidelines wondering what just happened.

I love that because it reminds me that I am not the only apple of God's eye. Even when I think I am safe in the security of my own tradition, God is greater—greater than my book, greater than my tradition, greater than my need to be right. While that may be upsetting at first it is also very freeing, to be reminded that there is always something new for me to learn about the spaciousness of God's heart, which has room in it for a lot more people than I think.

The story of the Good Samaritan is one of those stories, although it has been told so often to such self-serving ends that I am not sure anyone can really hear it anymore. The Bible never calls it the story of the Good Samaritan, for one thing. If your Bible has that heading, then an editor put it there—to help you find it, maybe, or to give you the punch line at the beginning so you would not have to expend too much energy figuring out what the story is about.

The problem with the heading is that the story itself has changed the way most people think of Samaritans. They're good, right? Why else is the hospital across the waterway called the Good Samaritan Medical Center? Why do we have Good Samaritan laws to protect people who stop to help hurt strangers? The story of the Good Samaritan has defined the word "Samaritan" for people who would not recognize a real Samaritan if they bumped into one on the street. That sucks the punch right out of the story, because when Jesus first told it, his hearers thought of Samaritans as anything but good.

But let's start where the story starts. Call it the story of the Argumentative Lawyer. How many of you are lawyers, by the way? My sister is too—corporate litigation—so I promise not to pile on. The lawyer in this story is just doing his job. At the beginning of it, he could be any of us. By the end of it, he is all of us. He just wants Jesus to tell him the truth about how things work with God.

"What must I do to inherit eternal life?" the lawyer asks Jesus—or as we say in North Georgia, "What must I do to be saved?" Luke says the man was testing Jesus, but it's not a bad thing to test people who claim to speak for God, and the lawyer's question is a good one to ask any preacher. "What must I do to inherit eternal life?"

If a preacher says, "Open your wallet and give me all your money," then you might want to think twice about going back to that church. Or if a preacher says, "Look deep into my eyes and repeat after me," then I don't think I'd go there either. But Jesus did not say either of those things. Instead, he asked the lawyer to think for himself.

"'What is written in the law?'" he asked the man. "'What do you read there?'" (v. 26). This is standard rabbinical practice, by the way. There's a Woody Allen story about the man who asked his rabbi, "Why does a rabbi always answer a question with a question?" The rabbi thought for a moment and said, "Why shouldn't a rabbi always answer a question with a question?"

This may be frustrating for people who want straight answers from their spiritual leaders that will help them feel more secure about themselves, but it is also a very good way to teach. By bouncing the lawyer's question back to him, Jesus not only made the man think for himself; he also found out what the man believed.

"You shall love the Lord your God with all your heart, and with all your soul, and with all your strength, and with all your mind," the lawyer answered him, "and your neighbor as yourself" (v. 27). Some of you know this as the Great Commandment— a combination of verses from the books of Deuteronomy and Leviticus—and you probably thought that Jesus was the one who said it. That is because he *did*, in the Gospels according to Mark and Matthew, but for some reason Luke put the Great Commandment in the lawyer's mouth instead—maybe to remind us that God's wisdom can come into the world through *any* of us, not just our spiritual leaders. Or maybe he did it to remind us that just because we know right answers and can say them out loud does not mean that we have ever tried putting them into practice.

"'You have given the right answer,'" Jesus says to the lawyer, "'*do* this, and you will live'" (v. 28).

So there is a straight answer to the man's question: if he will actually *do* what he knows is right—if he will *do* love—then he can start living eternal life anytime he wants. He does not have to sell all that he owns and give the proceeds to the poor (that's a different story). He does not have to take up his cross and follow Jesus (that's a different story too). In this story, all the man has to do is love God with all his heart, soul, strength, and mind, and his neighbor as himself. If he will do that, then he will live.

But the lawyer, who set out to test Jesus and is now feeling like he's the one being tested, tries to save face by asking for a definition of terms. You know how that works, right? When someone asks you a question and you give your best possible answer—but you can tell from the person's raised eyebrows that there is some question about your follow-through—you can sometimes buy yourself a little time by seeking clarification. Exactly *whom* you are supposed to be doing *what* for, under what kind of *circumstances*, for approximately how *long?* Lawyers aren't the only ones who do this for a living.

"And who is my neighbor?" (v. 29), the lawyer asks, which is when Jesus decides this guy needs to hear a story more than he needs to finish his deposition. It's going to be a teaching story, too, which means that it is going to end with another question. What did you expect? But at least that way the lawyer will have to come up with his own answer instead of leaning on Jesus to give him one for free.

So Jesus launches into the now-famous story about the relative neighborliness of a priest, a Levite, and a Samaritan who come across a hurt man left half dead by robbers on the side of a road. The success of the story depends entirely on how Jesus' audience views these three kinds of people. Since most of us view the priest and the Levite as Jews, it's important to remember that everyone who first heard the story was Jewish. That's not the point. The point is how the characters respond to the person in the ditch.

Whatever else Jesus' listeners thought about priests and Levites in those days, they knew that both of them worked in the temple and this put them pretty high up on the holiness scale. Priests and Levites handled holy things. They performed sacred rituals. They helped people present their sacrifices to God at the holiest place on earth. So I think it's safe to say that both the priest and the Levite in this story would have been regarded as pretty observant people, who knew what it meant to do things right.

The Samaritan was way down at the other end of the scale. While he and his people worshiped the same God the priests and Levites did, they rejected two-thirds of the Hebrew Bible as false teaching. They saw the temple in Jerusalem as a disgrace. They had their own temple on Mount Gerazim, with their own separate priesthood, which people in Jerusalem saw as an elaborate sham. These two people really did not like each other. They were heretics in each other's eyes.

Plus, this particular Samaritan seems to be a trader—one of the most despised ways to earn a living in those days—who bought wine and olive oil cheap in Jerusalem and sold them at a premium down in Jericho. Why else did he have so much money on him, and why was he so well known to the innkeeper on the road between those two places? The only people who stayed at inns were people who had no family or friends to take them in.

One year my husband, Ed, and I had to spend Christmas Eve at a Motel 8 on I-95 during a blizzard, eating recently thawed turkey dinners in a dining room with about seven other transients. Imagine our $39 room and you'll know where the Samaritan spent the night while he was on the road between Jerusalem and Jericho.

This was the last guy in the world the lawyer wanted to choose as the hero of the story, but what else could he do? After the priest had crossed the road to avoid helping the beaten man in the ditch and the lower-ranking Levite had done the same thing, there was no one left standing but the—ugh—Samaritan, whose name the lawyer could not even bring himself to say out loud. When Jesus finally got around to asking the question at the end of the teaching story—"'Which of these three, do you think, was a neighbor to the man who fell into the hands of the robbers?'" (v. 36)—the lawyer could not make himself say the "S" word. "The one who showed him mercy" (v. 37), he said instead, using five words where one would have sufficed.

This is not a story meant to help us feel better about ourselves. This is a story designed to do brain surgery on us, opening up the possibility that we have our good guys and our bad guys all mixed up. None of us really know what is inside another person. We may think we know, based on how our people and their people have treated each other in the past, but we do not know. We are all capable of surprising each other, every single day, and a single act of kindness has the power to call a whole history of against-ness into question. By inventing a story in which that happened, Jesus put "good" and "Samaritan" together in his hearers' minds for the first time. He knew that sometimes you have to start telling a different kind of story before a different kind of future can unfold.

This is not a story meant to help us feel better about ourselves. This is a story designed to do brain surgery on us, opening up the possibility that we have our good guys and our bad guys all mixed up.

A. J. Levine, a Jewish professor of New Testament at Vanderbilt, says that if Jesus had been a Samaritan, he would have told the story of the Good Jew. The best way to recover the punch of the parable, she says, is to imagine the hero of it as the last person in the world you want to call "good." Try moving it to the West Bank, she says, since that is where the ancient kingdom of Samaria once was. Make the man in the ditch an Israeli Jew. After a rabbi and a member of the Israeli Knesset have passed him by, imagine a Muslim member of Hamas bending down to bind the man's wounds, bathe him, and make sure he is taken care of. "If that scenario could be imagined by anyone in the Middle East," Levine concludes, perhaps there might be more hope for peace."[1]

I don't know about you, but as a young Christian I was taught to get my beliefs in order before I did things. Before I went out with a boy, I should be sure I knew what I believed about right relationships between girls and boys. Before I engaged someone of another faith in conversation, I should be sure I knew what I believed about that person's salvation. Before I spent my paycheck, I should make sure I knew what I believed about giving back to God.

In many ways, that was great advice. But based on the story of the Good Samaritan, I wonder if things don't work the other way around. Maybe our lives are designed to upset our beliefs, not to reinforce them. Maybe it is a better idea to *let our lives teach us what to believe* instead of *making our lives conform to our beliefs*—because if you had asked the man in the ditch what he believed about who would help him—the clergyman and the deacon of his own faith or the despised foreigner—he would have gotten it all wrong. He would have given the wrong answer. It was not until later, when he was lying in a clean bed in an inn down the road with his bill paid in advance, that he had time to revise that answer, updating his beliefs to match his experience. *A good Samaritan!* Who would have thought?

Maybe the only belief any of us really needs is that compassion is the way of life—or love, if you prefer—not a *feeling* but an *action*, the way God acts toward us and the way God calls us to act toward one another, with power to change the world one ditch at a time. I don't know how you pull that off here in Palm Beach, but you'll think of something. Because given the choice between passing by on the other side and being moved to act with compassion, the right answer is clear as a bell. *Do* love and you will live.

Royal Poinciana Chapel,[*]
Palm Beach, Florida
Second Sunday after the Epiphany
January 19, 2014

[*]An earlier version of this sermon was given at Riverside Church in New York City in 2013.

Chapter Thirteen

Rich in Love

Mark 10:17–31

*Then Jesus looked around and said to his disciples, "How hard it
will be for those who have wealth to enter the kingdom of God!"
And the disciples were perplexed at these words. But Jesus said to
them again, "Children, how hard it is to enter the kingdom of God!
It is easier for a camel to go through the eye of a needle than for
someone who is rich to enter the kingdom of God."*
—Mark 10:23–25

Good morning, Chautauqua, and welcome to week two, where
the theme is money and power. It's a great week to be a chaplain,
especially a Christian one, since Jesus said more about money
than he ever said about war, sex, or religion—though the only
times the money passages really come up in church are during
stewardship season. So I thought I'd sneak up on some of those
stories right here in the dead heat of July, with no pledge cards
in your pews—surprise them with an early wake-up call to see
if they had anything unexpected to say when they weren't being
recruited for the usual purposes.

The story of the rich young ruler seems like the place to start,
not only because it shows up in all three of the Synoptic Gospels
but also because it gets straight to the point: "'How hard it will be

for those who have wealth to enter the kingdom of God!'" If you know the story well, then those words come fully illustrated, with the picture of an overloaded camel stalled in front of an impossibly slender passageway with no hope of getting through—hilarious to those who don't own camels, distressing to those who do. During stewardship season, a friendly preacher will usually assure you that generosity is all God asks. Offload a bag or two of that camel's burden for the good of the kingdom and trust God to take care of the rest.

That's not a *terrible* lesson to take from the story. It's just that the way Mark tells it is so much more *interesting* than that. In the first place, the man who comes up to Jesus is not identified as a rich young ruler. He's just a man, Mark says—though a truly remarkable man, as it turns out—the only person in Mark's Gospel whom Jesus is said to love. He's also the only person in this Gospel who turns down Jesus' invitation to follow, which seems to hurt him worse than it hurts anyone else. The only mention of his wealth comes at the very end of the story, when he is already walking away from Jesus with his heart in tatters. So when Jesus follows the whole thing up with the picture of the stuck camel, the disciples don't think it's hilarious at all. They are astounded instead. If not this good man, whom Jesus thought well enough of to make one of them, then who can be saved?

Because clearly, the man can't be—not now that he has turned Jesus down, not now that he has decided to go back to his old well-padded life instead of choosing the new stripped-down life Jesus offered him. Whatever the disciples thought of the man when he first landed on his knees in front of Jesus, he has become a camel in their minds, raising great big poofs of dust under his feet as he turns from the kingdom and lumbers his way back home.

That's the easiest thing to do with the man, after all. Make him a bad man in some way— a self-righteous man, a greedy man, a man addicted to his comforts—anything that will make him worse than the rest of us (who also have many possessions) so we can read his story in some kind of peace. But what if he's *not* a bad man? What if he's the very *best* kind of man, so that his goodness is at least as serious a problem for him as his wealth?

Mark provides some clues. For starters, he lets us know that this man is no casual seeker. He does not *walk* toward Jesus. He *runs*, and when he gets there, he drops to his knees to ask his burning question: "'Good Teacher, what must I do to inherit eternal life?'" (v. 7). Jesus has been asked plenty of questions that start like this with tricks and hooks hidden inside, but this does not seem to be one of them. The man did not arrive with an entourage, for one thing. There are no witnesses standing around recording everything on their cell phones. You also have to give Jesus some credit for being able to read a person's character. The man with the upturned face wants to know what he has to do to live in God's presence forever and he believes Jesus can tell him. There's not a trace of deceit.

The only unusual thing about the man's question is the word he puts in front of "Teacher." People use that title for Jesus all the time in the Gospels—forty-nine times, to be exact, no matter what translation you use—but this man is the only one to put a qualifier in front of it: not just "Teacher" but "Good Teacher." Make of that what you will. I think it's the most complimentary thing he can think of to say to Jesus, which tells me what high value this man places on goodness. *Good* Teacher. It's the gift he wants to give Jesus before he asks something in return, but Jesus will not accept it.

"'Why do you call me good?'" (v. 18). Jesus asks the man kneeling in front of him. Maybe he helps the man up at that point, waiting a second while he dusts off his knees. "'No one is good but God alone'" (v. 18).

That line has bothered Christians for so long. *Is Jesus saying he's not good? Is he saying he's not God?* They are relevant questions, but I don't think Jesus is thinking of Trinitarian doctrine at the moment. I think he's noticing what is most important to this man and messing with it—turning over the man's linguistic tables, as it were—by suggesting that no one on this earth, not even this particular Teacher, can possess or assign goodness to anyone else. God alone is good. God alone is God.

Since the man is sincere, he does not argue. He listens instead, as Jesus goes over the commandments—not all of them, but the ones about how humans are meant to treat other humans. If you have ever had trouble saying them in the right order, take heart. Jesus puts number five after number nine and adds an extra one just because he feels like it. He knows the man already knows the commandments, but if it's eternal life the man is after, it may be important for him to know that Jesus' answer is the same as Moses' answer: do this—do these—and you will live.

But the man has already done them. He has built up some spiritual muscle, in other words. He has devoted himself to a steady practice of goodness, and while he knows there is nothing easy about the life he has chosen, he does have reason to believe that he will be able to do whatever Jesus tells him to do next. He is ready. He is willing. He even signals how carefully he has listened to Jesus by dropping the modifier this time. "'Teacher,'" he says, when Jesus has finished reviewing the divine teachings, "'I have kept all these since my youth'" (v. 20).

That, Mark says, is when Jesus loves him—the only person in this whole Gospel whom Jesus is said to love. But loves him why? Because he is a true son of the covenant, just as Jesus is? Because he can say what he just said without the least stink of pride? Because having done *enough* is not enough for him—he wants to do *more*? Mark doesn't say, which is wise of him since the best kind of love has so little to do with "why." Still, what Jesus says next is revealing.

"'You lack one thing,'" he says to the good man who wants all the life there is; "'go, sell what you own, and give the money to the poor, and you will have treasure in heaven; then come, follow me'" (v. 21). Jesus is offering the man a chance to share his life—a spiritual proposal of the highest order—but Jesus has finally found something this man cannot do. He has put his finger on the one thing that the man with everything needs most, which is *less*.

Nothing is what this man lacks. He has everything else. His cup of blessing is full to overflowing. He has kept the commandments since his youth. Though we don't know it yet, he has many possessions. His well-fed camels wear bridles made of softest leather, with red and gold pom-poms crowning their heads. Like everything else under his care, they flourish. Up to this moment he thought he had all the resources he needed to do whatever Jesus told him to do, but *empty the cup and hand over the reins?* Abandon everything and everyone dependent on his care?

Just like that, the man knows he cannot do it. He cannot afford the life Jesus is offering him. As soon as the Teacher finishes speaking, the man turns without a word and walks away grieving, for—as Mark finally says—"he had many possessions" (v. 21).

Mark may have hid the detail, but Jesus makes a point of it. "'How hard it will be for those who have wealth to enter the kingdom of God'" (v. 23), he says to his disciples, who are so perplexed by the saying that he has to say it again, this time giving them the camel picture to go with it. Poor camel. Even if you could get rid of all the bags loaded with stuff, there would still be the ribs, the hump, the excessively long legs. There's simply no way through the needle for the likes of him. But go ahead and imagine it, Jesus says—because even *that* is easier than for someone who is rich to enter the kingdom of God.

Why didn't the disciples cheer out loud when they heard him say that? Two of them had left their fishing nets to follow him, after all. Two more had walked away from a fishing boat *with their father still in it.* Another had left a well-paid job as tax assessor, pushing his chair away from his desk to go with Jesus the moment Jesus asked. They had all walked away from something—they were all voluntarily poor—so you'd think they would have rejoiced when Jesus said what he said about the rich. Instead, they were astounded by it—*greatly* astounded, Mark says, without saying why. Was it because they still saw wealth as a sign of God's favor, no matter who had it or how it was used? Or was it because they were still holding out hope of some kind of riches for themselves?

"'Then who can be saved?'" they ask Jesus (v. 26). It's a very good question—essentially the same one the rich man asked Jesus back at the beginning of the story, which means that the rich man and the disciples may not be as different as they first appear.

Since the rich man is gone, he can't hear Jesus' answer, but Mark has written it down so we can. "'For mortals it is impossible, but not for God; for God all things are possible'" (v. 27), Jesus says, and nine times out of ten that's where the sermon ends. No one is getting through the eye of the needle on their own virtues, but God can do anything God wants. Amen.

Almost no one sticks around for Peter's self-interested little gaffe at the end, which is not only embarrassing but practically defines "anticlimax" after everything else that has transpired.

"So that means we're in, right?" Peter asks Jesus. This is not a direct translation from the Greek, but it's close. "I mean, look, we left everything and followed you, so we don't have anything to worry about, right? Sell all that you own: check. Give the proceeds to the poor: check. 'And you will have treasure in heaven.' That part was for us, right? And by the time we get there it is going to be *a lot*. Just checking to make sure I heard you right, sir."

You can tell Jesus is ready for a nap. He hasn't got much energy left to deconstruct Peter's question, so he placates his lead disciple the same way he might calm a child. *You'll get back a hundred times more than you gave up*, he tells Peter in so many words—*houses, brothers, sisters, mothers, children, fields with persecutions, eternal life in the age to come*. Wait, persecutions? *Yes, fields of them. Were persecutions not on your list of treasures, Peter? Maybe you're still holding on to something you need to let go.*

It's an odd exchange, but that's what makes me think this story is for more than rich people, and that the rich man's problem was more than money. He wanted to be good, just like Peter did. He wanted everything God had to offer, and he was willing to do whatever it took. He was as attached to his treasure on earth as Peter was attached to his treasure in heaven, but I don't think that made either of them bad. It just made them attached—to what they had, to what they could do. Jesus loved them too much to let them go on like that, thinking heaven was something they could secure for themselves—by giving up, by taking on, by following, by doing good.

Jesus loved them too much to let them go on like that, thinking heaven was something they could secure for themselves—by giving up, by taking on, by following, by doing good.

What must I do to inherit eternal life? *Oh, I'm so sorry. There's nothing, really. On earth, there's plenty to do. But at the level of eternity, God is the only doer.*

This is very subversive good news. Right up to the end it sounds like the rich man has failed to do the one thing he needs to do to inherit eternal life. The kingdom was his, and he failed to claim it. Jesus' love was his, and he failed to secure it. Then out comes the rug and it turns out no one can "do" any of that. No one can do it but God alone.

The man still loses his chance to share Jesus' life, which is reason enough for him to go away grieving, but he'll be rich in love for the rest of his life—because what Jesus gives, he never takes away—and the kingdom? For mortals it is impossible, but not for God; for God all things are possible.

The Chautauqua Institution,
Chautauqua, New York
July 4, 2016

Chapter Fourteen

The Parable of the Fearful Investor

Matthew 25:14–19

"For it is as if a man, going on a journey, summoned his slaves and entrusted his property to them; to one he gave five talents, to another two, to another one, to each according to his ability. Then he went away. The one who had received the five talents went off at once and traded with them, and made five more talents. In the same way, the one who had the two talents made two more talents. But the one who had received the one talent went off and dug a hole in the ground and hid his master's money."

—Matthew 25:14–19

This is the beginning of a well-worn parable that is told most often during stewardship season, apparently to convince listeners that even Jesus thinks their money would be better invested in the church than in a hole in the ground. But I am not at all sure the parable will serve the purpose it is so often recruited to serve, especially once you let it off the leash to see what *else* it might have to say about money and power.

Since we do not have the full text before us, let me remind you of the narrative Jesus invents to get to the punch line of his story. A man has just gotten home from a long journey, he says. Before the man left, he entrusted his servants with his property. He made them his money managers. When he finally returns home, the first thing he wants to know is not how they have been or whether any trees fell on the house while he was away, but how much more money they have made for him in his absence.

Two of his servants turn out to be successful investors. They have doubled his money, and he praises them accordingly. But when the third servant admits he was too afraid of his master to risk losing any of the money—that he buried it in the ground for safekeeping instead—the master exhibits the kind of behavior that lets us know why his servant was right to be afraid of him in the first place. He calls the servant names for failing to turn a profit, blames him for telling the truth about how mean the master is, then orders him thrown into outer darkness for his colossal lack of talent at banking.

This master is no Bill Gates. But since most of us have been taught that Jesus wants us to believe what the master says is true, we get busy finding something the third servant did *wrong* so the repellant master can be *right*. The last interpreter I heard decided that *fear* was the servant's fatal flaw. It was his *risk-aversion* that landed him in hell.

It was a pretty good guess, based on the last hundred years of biblical commentary. C. H. Dodd (1935): This is "a story of a man whom overcaution and cowardice led into a breach of trust." T. W. Manson (1949): "The punishment for neglected opportunity is deprivation of opportunity." Dan Via (1967): The third servant's refusal to risk led to repressed guilt, resulting in "the loss of the opportunity for meaningful existence." John Donahue (1988): "out of fear of failure, he refused even to try to succeed."[1] Any questions?

The unanimous weight of these verdicts reminded me of something I heard in a homeless shelter once, from a man who had been on the receiving end of a great deal of advice about how to get back on his feet. After being coached on handling his addiction, applying for jobs, managing his finances, and qualifying for low-income housing, he finally looked at the person most invested in his rehabilitation and said, "Why you want to fix me up and feed me back into the same machine that ground me up and spit me out in the first place?"

How you hear a parable has a lot to do with where you are hearing it *from*.

Back in the 1980s, the Catholic Foreign Missionary Society of America published a four-volume Bible commentary called *The Gospel in Solentiname*. As some of you know, Solentiname is a place name, a remote archipelago on Lake Nicaragua inhabited by subsistence-level farmers and fishers. A lay monastery called Our Lady of Solentiname flourished there in the 1970s on one of its thirty-eight islands—the living vision of a pastor named Ernesto Cardenal.

On Sundays the priest in the black beret invited the *campesinos* of Solentiname to meet with him to talk about the Gospel reading for the week—not after the sermon, but in place of the sermon. It was such an unusual idea that people came. Those with boats rowed to meet with him while those who did not stayed home to wait for the reports, but the meetings themselves became legendary.

By one account[2] as many as a thousand people showed up to proclaim the gospel in Solentiname—young and old, male and female, literate and illiterate. Across all their differences, what they had in common was life below the poverty line and the revolution going on around them—a popular uprising against then-president Somoza, whose family controlled 40 percent of Nicaragua's economy and 30 percent of the country's arable land.[3]

You can't visit the monastery chapel today, I'm afraid, because in 1977 the National Guard of Nicaragua burned it down. But you can read the commentaries that were produced there, including one on the parable of the Talents. On the Sunday it came up, a Colombian poet named William started the discussion by saying, "That's a lousy parable." Unfazed, Pastor Cardenal asked him why it was lousy. Here are some choice bits from the discussion that followed:

WILLIAM: "Because it's about speculating with money: something we all condemn, like putting money out at interest; giving the money to others so they can work and work with it and hand over the profits to the owner of the money."

[ERNESTO]: "It's really a very ugly example that Jesus gives of exploitation, of speculation with money, of pure capitalism."

ADAN: "Well, he probably didn't say it. Who knows who said it?" . . .

WILLIAM: "Well, I don't know. Besides, the example is lousier because of what the servant says who hid the money: that he was a hard master, that he gathered where he hadn't put anything, that he harvested and didn't sow."

TERESITA; his wife: "At that time there were only masters and servants, right? He had to talk like that so they'd understand. At that time all the servants had to be working with the master's talents or money, and that's why he had to give that example."

[ERNESTO]: "He was seeing the exploitation there was in the society of his time, and that's going on now—much worse with the banks and finances of today."

WILLIAM: "There's the bank, there's a bank there!"[4]

Since you keep up with the news I won't give you the latest figures on how many U.S. banks hold what percentage of our country's gross domestic product, or the size of the average pay gap between American CEOs and their workers (except to say that it's in the neighborhood of $12 million—for two people in the same company who live under the same sun and breathe the same air).

In Jesus' day, a talent weighed close to a hundred pounds[5] and was worth twenty years of an ordinary person's labor. The only people who had that kind of money were the wealthy few, whose households were the basic economic units of the time. How did they make the money? In the usual ways: they engaged in trade, got goods to market, ran import-export businesses, lent money to people at interest—especially land-poor people, who often had trouble trying to make ends meet during a long drought or a catastrophic illness in the family.

Wealthy householders were happy to "help" in hard times. There was nothing to it. If you were strapped for cash, you got the best interest rate you could, you put up your land as collateral, and you got busy bringing in the sheaves. By the time you figured out what 60 percent interest really meant, it was too late. Your land went into foreclosure, and quicker than you could say "Leviticus" it wasn't yours anymore. But that didn't always mean you had to leave. You could stay if you were willing to work for your former lender—if you could stand to watch the fields you picked every rock out of by hand being repurposed as olive groves or vineyards, crops more easily monetized, which would appeal to a more upscale market both at home and abroad.[6]

Since "abroad" was where first-century financiers often had to be, they employed household retainers to look after things while they were gone—"slaves," maybe, but well-placed ones—domestic bureaucrats in charge of managing workers, keeping books, collecting debts, who were also free to make something for themselves on the side once they had seen to their master's interests. Their share in such "honest graft" reflected their own standing in the household. The higher-ups were entrusted with more than the lower-downs, but as far as the master was concerned, the more the merrier, since there were that many more people to keep eyes on each other while he was away.

Whatever the servants' standing, their dependence on the master was built into the system. They lived on his excess. The better he did, the better they did. Their wealth came from his. If he wanted to spend his money on nice suits and big houses, there was no public shame in that. It helped, actually. Like good advertisement, it let prospective clients know how capable he really was. Wealth attracted wealth. It was its own justification. A master who shared a little venture capital with his retainers when he went out of town was not only increasing his potential joy. He was inviting them into it as well. ""Well done, good and trustworthy slave; you have been trustworthy in a few things, I will put you in charge of many things; enter into the joy of your master"'" (v. 21).

But here's what I want to know: when did we decide that the man going on a journey in the parable of the Talents was *God*? I know Jesus told it as a parable of the kingdom, but how does that turn the little "m" master in the story into the capital "M" Master of the cosmos? Haven't there always been a lot of masters applying for God's job, and not all of them good?

If you read the parable like someone living on a lake in Nicaragua—or like one of the "little ones" who followed Jesus around—it's hard to see the master as anything but one more tycoon sitting on a pile of money so high that he cannot see the bottom of it—which is why he has to hire people to keep it flowing up from wherever it comes from without troubling him with too many details. As long as they can double his money, they are welcome to make it any way they like. As long as they can give him back twice as much as he gave them, they may deduct their "expenses" to the full extent of the law—which has been generously amended so that people like the master can go on stimulating the economy for the good of all.

Seriously?

We are seriously supposed to believe that the first two servants in this parable are the praiseworthy ones, both in this world and the next—for making a wealthy man wealthier, for keeping an absentee landlord in business, for scoring a 100 percent rate of return for him in return for their own piece of the pie? These are the guys who are doing it right, while the third guy—the only one who buries the money where it can't do any more harm, the only one who tells the truth about the master, the only one who refuses to play the exploitation game any longer even if it means being banished from his master's expensive "joy"—he is the one whose "overcaution" and "cowardice" have cost him "the opportunity for meaningful existence"?

I can only imagine what William from Solentiname would say about that. Of course the master threw the third guy out! He couldn't have someone in his household exposing the truth "that he gathered where he hadn't put anything, that he harvested and didn't sow." And that outer darkness where there is "wailing and gnashing of teeth"? I'm pretty sure William would want to know if you really believe that darkness is God's own hell, or if it's just where whistle-blowers go once they decide they can't go on the way they have been going anymore. They may not even have to be thrown there—they may simply decide they'd rather join the 99 percent in the dark than stay with the 1 percent who burn through all the brightness without ever seeing those who foot the bill.

Maybe you have read about Dignity Village in Portland, Oregon—a community of formerly homeless people who started out fourteen years ago in tents and now have a contract with the city that allows them to live in forty-three tiny, handmade houses on land that Portland calls a campground. It's no Solentiname, but longtime resident Lisa Larson says, "It's family here, a dysfunctional family, and there are times . . . we fight like cats and dogs, but if you are lonely and stick your head out the door, and holler, somebody will be there."[7]

If any of the villagers have hundred-pound talents, they are definitely buried. Each of them pays thirty-five dollars a month to live in Dignity, and each of them works ten hours a week to keep the place going. They also have a small recycling and firewood business, but last year's operating budget was still less than $27,000—not enough to finance the transition from portable to flushing toilets, after fourteen years.

In light of this morning's parable, I've been trying to imagine Jesus walking up to Lisa and saying, "I'm baaaaack. Now where's my profit? I invested in you, remember? So what are you still doing here? Afraid? What do you mean you were *afraid*? Hey! Someone take all Lisa's stuff and give her house to someone who already has one. Then get this worthless nobody out of here and let's get back to business."

You know what? I can't imagine it. I can't imagine it at all.

William's right: It's a lousy parable, and it seems entirely possible to me that Jesus is deeply disappointed in our willingness to swallow it whole, without even clearing our throats to say that the God we know has never run a household like that and never will. The God we worship is not that kind of master. The God we worship *exposes* that kind of master.

It's a lousy parable, and it seems entirely possible to me that Jesus is deeply disappointed in our willingness to swallow it whole, without even clearing our throats to say that the God we know has never run a household like that and never will. The God we worship is not that kind of master. The God we worship *exposes* that kind of master.

So maybe this isn't a sermon about the parable of the Talents at all. Maybe it's a sermon about how we read Scripture instead—about why we are so reluctant to challenge established meanings, about what we think is at risk if we do. Above all, maybe it's about what might happen if we stopped thinking of the truth of Scripture as something *already set down in a book* and reconceived it as something that happens *when we get together around that book*, letting the sharp edges on the page rub up against the sharp edges of our lives until they both yield new and living truth. We might even be able to do it in a way that helps a few harsh masters relax.

Wouldn't that be something?

The Chautauqua Institution,
Chautauqua, New York
July 6, 2016

Chapter Fifteen

The Widow's Might

Mark 12:41–44

He sat down opposite the treasury, and watched the crowd putting money into the treasury. Many rich people put in large sums. A poor widow came and put in two small copper coins, which are worth a penny. Then he called his disciples and said to them, "Truly I tell you, this poor widow has put in more than all those who are contributing to the treasury. For all of them have contributed out of their abundance; but she out of her poverty has put in everything she had, all she had to live on."

—Mark 12:41–44

If you know your Bible, you know about God and widows. From the Torah to the Psalms to the Prophets and the Gospels, God makes special provision for widows and their children, commanding humans to do the same. Famous biblical widows include Tamar, Judith, Ruth, Naomi, Orpah, and Anna, plus many more who star in stories that don't tell us their names. The widow of Zarephath and the widow in today's story both fall in that category—two women who are often paired during stewardship season for giving every last scrap of the little bit they had to God.

When the widow of Zarephath did it, she got her own miraculous feeding in the wilderness—a jar of meal that never emptied, a jug of oil that never failed—on which she, the prophet Elijah, and her whole household ate for many days. The widow of Jerusalem's reward was less tangible but no less significant. She got Jesus' attention, who called his disciples to pay attention to her too—the kind of person who usually slips right under the radar, dropping her last two coins into the temple treasury.

It was all she had to live on, Jesus said. How did he know? Maybe the same way he knew things about other people from a distance without ever having to ask. Or maybe it was written all over her, for anyone who really looked at her to read: the way she held her ground in front of the treasury while more substantial people came and went; the way she prayed over the coins before she let go of them like a gambler blowing on dice, then stood there a long time after they had fallen from her hand, letting the full weight of what she had just done sink in. *So this is what "penniless" feels like.*

I have always imagined her old, but Mark doesn't say so. She could have been twenty-three, with two kids under five at home. All Mark says about her is that she was a "poor widow." This may be a first-century redundancy—like saying she was a powerless woman or a broke pauper—or it may be a reminder that not all widows in those days were poor. Under Roman law, widows could inherit from their husbands and manage their own property. By all accounts, Paul might not have had the paper to write his letters on without the generosity of the wealthy widows who supported him.

But those women are usually named, and this one is not. She is not a rich widow and she is not a poor married woman. She is a poor widow—the worst possible combination—so that young or old, she lives her life on the bottom rung of every ladder that goes anywhere in her world. Her insignificance has as much to do with her bank account as her gender. She is as invisible in the temple as she is in the marketplace. With nothing to spend and no one to speak up for her, she is not a person of interest—not to the treasurer and not to the turnip-seller. She is just in the way. She is just using up air.

Yet she is the one who catches Jesus' attention—on his last trip to God's house, in what will turn out to be the last week of his life. According to Mark, this poor widow is the subject of one of his last teachings to his disciples before he leaves the temple for the last time.

Jesus isn't looking for her when he sees her. He is sitting opposite the treasury all by himself watching people come and go. He sees rich people putting in large sums. He probably sees some people making a show of putting something in without actually doing it. Who's to know whether there's anything in that envelope or not? Then he sees her—the poor widow—and he watches what she does.

There is nothing to it, really. It only takes Mark half a sentence to describe: she puts in two small copper coins, which are worth a penny. Then Jesus calls his disciples over to make sure they don't miss what has just happened—though they may be excused for wondering why it is such a big deal. Since when did Jesus start keeping track of people's pledges?

Then Jesus tells them why it is a big deal—because this woman has just set her death in motion right there in front of him. She has just committed economic suicide by pitching her last two coins into a treasure box so heavy that she cannot even hear her coins clink when they go inside. Whatever she thinks the money inside that box is used for, it is used to pay bills, which makes her gift as negligible as she is. It will cost the temple more to count her two coins than the coins can buy. A receipt costs more than a penny.

Her final gesture is entirely futile, in other words. It won't make a bit of difference—or at least it wouldn't have, if she hadn't had a witness. But she has a witness, who does more than see what she is doing. He also puts words to her desperate act. *The others will never miss what they gave*, he says to his disciples, *but she—she gave everything she had to live on. Out of the nothing she had, she gave it all away.* He alone can see what she is really doing. She is not just offering up her last two coins. She is offering up her life.

In churches all around the world, Jesus' words are construed as praise of the widow, usually in the context of asking people to give as generously as she did—especially people who have so little to spare that they fear their gifts may be as negligible as hers was. *Give what you can. Every gift counts. Your two coins mean as much to God as a five-figure check from someone else. What you give to God, God will give back to you.*

But there are at least two things wrong with that, which I think would leap out at anyone if we read whole pages of Scripture in church and not just select bits. First, Jesus does not commend the widow's pattern of giving to anyone else. There is no "go and do likewise" here, no "God loves a cheerful giver." That is not the moral of this story. Second, there is nothing to suggest that Jesus sees her offering as an offering to God.

One second before he sat down opposite the temple treasury, Mark says, Jesus denounced the scribes who made their living off of women like her. "They devour widow's houses" (v. 40), Jesus says. How did they do that? Mark doesn't say, but in those days scribes were the learned people—the literate ones who knew Torah well enough to draw up contracts and wills, file taxes, decide legal cases—think accountant, lawyer, judge, and preacher all rolled up into one—which made them very valuable members of society.

Since you are learned people yourselves, you know that the Jewishness of the scribes is not the issue here. Jesus was Jewish, all of his disciples were Jewish, most of the people in the temple were Jewish, and the poor widow was Jewish. This is a Jewish story, not a story about Jews. It is a *human* story about valuable members of society who use their education and their professional status to their own advantage (isn't that the point?) even when that sometimes leads them to take advantage of less valuable members of society.

No one knows for sure what Jesus meant about the scribes "devouring widow's houses." Maybe they offered to help not-yet-poor widows manage their husband's estates, subtracting a percentage of the assets in exchange for their trusteeship. Maybe they advised the women on charitable giving that would improve the scribes' own social standing in the community. Or maybe they did their devouring from a distance—not by taking direct advantage of the women but by interpreting the law so that other people could do it without too great a toll on their consciences.

All it would take was a little editing. You could just focus on the parts of Scripture that focus on loving God with all your heart, soul, and might (Deut. 6:5) and leave out the part about loving the stranger as yourself (Lev. 19:34). You could offer a six-week series on the Ten Commandments and leave out all the complicated commandments about leaving grapes in your field or olives on your trees so the aliens, the widows, and the orphans have something to eat (Deut. 24:20–21). Biblically literate people have a certain advantage, after all. Ordinary people can't spend all day poring over the text, and even if they could, half of them would gladly pay you to *just tell them what it says.*

I don't know what the problem with the scribes was, but whatever it was, Jesus was really mad about it—so mad that after he saw what the poor widow did with her last two coins he walked out of the temple and told his disciples that the whole place was coming down. He had to interrupt them, too, since they were busy admiring the scenery. "'Look, Teacher,'" one of them said to him, "'what large stones and what large buildings!'" (Mark 13:1).

Maybe they were gawking because they had never been to Jerusalem before, or maybe it was because the temple complex was undergoing major renovation. It was one of Herod the Great's big building projects—still underway forty years after Herod's death, with another thirty to go—which meant the whole place was a construction site during Jesus' entire public ministry. The temple itself was finished, though—plated pure gold, Josephus says, so that those who saw it at a distance said it looked like a fiery mountain covered with snow.[1]

"'Do you see these great buildings?'" Jesus asks his gaping disciples—just two verses after he has asked them to come see the poor widow feeding the temple treasury inside. "'Not one stone will be left here upon another; all will be thrown down'" (v. 2).

If you remove the brackets around the widow—if you listen to Jesus denounce the scribes for devouring widow's houses, then follow him over to see what she is doing with her last two cents, then follow him outside to pronounce judgment on the system that she has just funded—then it is really, really hard to hear what Jesus says about her as praise. It sounds a whole lot more like lament instead.

Whatever that poor woman was up to—committing economic suicide in the holiest place she could think of, trying to get God's attention, hoping she, like the widow of Zarephath, might go home to discover a jar of meal that never emptied, a jug of oil that never failed—she offered all that she had to an institution that was not worthy of her, and Jesus noticed.

She may even have been the deal-breaker, for him, the living-and-soon-to-be-dying proof that the system had lost its way, caring more for its own preservation than for the negligible people like her that it had been created to protect. Where were the scribes then—or the preachers now—to remind people of that?

"You shall not deprive a resident alien or an orphan of justice; you
     shall not take a widow's garment in pledge." (Deut. 24:17)
     "Learn to do good;
seek justice,
     rescue the oppressed,
defend the orphan,
     plead for the widow." (Isa. 1:17)
"The LORD tears down the house of the proud,
     but maintains the widow's boundaries. (Prov. 15:25)

On Jesus' last visit to God's house, in what would turn out to be the last week of his life, it was too late for him to fix all of that, so he did what he could. He called his disciples over to see something no one else in the room could see: a destitute woman invisible to everyone around her who had just passed through the eye of the needle. She slid right through, without one cent in her pocket to clink against the sides, leaving the scribes behind her to devour what was left of her house.

He called his disciples over to see something no one else in the room could see: a destitute woman invisible to everyone around her who had just passed through the eye of the needle. She slid right through, without one cent in her pocket to clink against the sides, leaving the scribes behind her to devour what was left of her house.

Within the week Jesus would be right behind her, which may be one more reason why he noticed her. There was something familiar about her—not just the end-of-the-line look on her face, or the way she hesitated while the coins were still in her hand. Was she hoping the cup might pass her by, that legions of angels might swoop down to rescue her? There was also the surprise on her face once she had dropped the coins into the treasury—a look of freedom, almost—as if she knew she had done all she could and the rest was up to God.

I know Christians who like to make this a story about Jesus' judgment on the temple—but that's a reading from the outside, not the inside. Stay inside the story and it's easy to see that Jesus' judgment fell on those who had *corrupted* the temple, not on the temple itself. The building project was Herod's, not God's. When Jesus started turning over tables, it was to drive out those who were buying and selling in the temple, not those who were coming to give themselves away. Jesus loved God's house, just like the poor widow did. Why else were they there?

There's a little building project going on at Chautauqua too, in case you hadn't noticed. I hadn't planned on giving a stewardship sermon this morning, but if you have a chance to give, I hope you will give generously. I hope you will keep this place alive and well so that people can come here for the food they need to practice the gospel in the world. Of course I also hope that if you see a poor widow filling out the last check in her checkbook for zero dollars and two cents, you will find some gracious way to handle that, now that Jesus has made people like her impossible to ignore.

Above all, I hope that together we can figure out how to be the best possible scribes—since that is who most of us are, really—the learned people, the people with power to spare, who are presented every day with at least half a dozen choices between securing our own safety or the safety of those with no power at all.

God has entrusted us with the teaching of the gospel—and more than that—with its embodiment, which includes protecting the vulnerable bodies all around us every day. The good news is that we have everything we need to do that: the grace of our Lord Jesus Christ, the love of God, and the fellowship of the Holy Spirit. May they be with us all forevermore.

The Chautauqua Institution,[*]
Chautauqua, New York
July 5, 2016

---

*An earlier version of this sermon was given at Morningside Presbyterian Church in Atlanta in 2009.

Chapter Sixteen

Divine Evolution

Sirach 24:1–12; John 1:1–18

In the beginning was the Word, and the Word was with God, and the Word was God. He was in the beginning with God. All things came into being through him, and without him not one thing came into being. What has come into being in him was life, and the life was the light of all people.

—John 1:1–4

This is John's birth narrative, which explains why there are no Christmas pageants based on it. The stories Matthew and Luke tell are full of things you can put costumes on: shepherds, angels, wise men, sheep. They are full of things you can paint on the backdrop: a stable, a manger, a guiding star overhead. We love them because they stay put, coming out of storage once a year with their invitation to remember a holy night long ago when all was calm, all was bright. They let us be children again, before putting our heavy coats back on and heading into a world that is going who-knows-where, with a bunch of swollen egos changing the script every 24-hour news cycle.

But there is no Bethlehem in John's Gospel, no holy family, no inn with no room, no manger. There's not even a baby in this story, because John's nativity begins before any of those things existed. It begins "in the beginning," the same way the Bible does. It begins with the Big Bang of God's Word, bringing the world into being one utterance at a time.

In the Genesis story there were six days full of words. "God said, 'Let there be light'; and there was light" (Gen. 1:3). After that came day, night, sky, earth, seas, plants, and planets. After that came living creatures of every kind, including humankind. All God had to do was *say* them and there they *were*: fish, birds, wild animals, creeping things, earthlings. They all came forth on the breath of God, taking shape through the power of God's creative Word.

But if you're thinking of phonics and sound waves, you're thinking too small. You might try thinking of "the Logos" instead, since that's the term John used and it's not as tame as "the Word." In the world of Genesis, God's Logos is God's agency, God's dynamic intelligence entering the cosmos like a meteor, taking on shape as it passes from the unbounded dimension of eternity into the bounded atmosphere of earth. God's Logos is God's rocket ship of self-revelation, the manifestation of God's divine reason and creativity in the material realm, where it both brings things into being and then holds them together so they don't fly apart.

John didn't invent the term. Greek and Jewish philosophers used it before him, and they weren't referring to Jesus when they did. But John made the connection for his Christian community and it stuck. From his time to ours, Christians identify the Logos as the Christ, the dynamic agency and intelligence of God that came to earth in the flesh. His human name was Jesus. He landed in Galilee. It was a whole new beginning, but how was John going to write about that? A manger was too small to contain the divine Logos. Shepherds were a dime a dozen. Even Mary, God bless her, was so *provincial*. So John did not include any of that in his story. He wrote a cosmic story instead—a second Genesis—about the preexistent Logos who was with God in the beginning, long before there was a Bethlehem, a Caesar, or a single star in the sky.

In John's birth story, the Logos is singular and it does not come out of God's mouth, at least not at first. The Logos is *with* God.

The Logos *is* God. It both is and isn't God, which may be why it doesn't have a name in the beginning—because it is not yet separate from God. God is bound to put breath behind the Word soon, because for some unknown reason God does not love being alone. God loves company. God loves "being with." How else did God know that Adam needed a partner, that it was not good for him to be alone? But there is no Adam in John's origin story yet. There is no Jesus. There is not even a world. There is just this primordial intimacy between God and God's Logos—God's dynamic energy, wanting to *become* something, even if that means leaving the divine womb and entering a too-bright cosmos full of loud noises, hard surfaces, and the smell of blood.

Before that happens, however, John wants to make sure we understand several crucial things. The first is the Logos' relationship to darkness ("The light shines in the darkness, and the darkness did not overcome it," 1:5). The second is the Logos' relationship to John the Baptizer ("He himself was not the light, but he came to testify to the light," v. 8). The third is the nature of the Logos' birth ("not of blood or of the will of the flesh or of the will of man, but of God," v. 13).

There is no need for a gender reveal. The Logos has been "he" from the start, since John already knows whom he is talking about, but he still takes his time getting to the verse that passes for a birth in his story: "And the Word became flesh and lived among us," he says at last, "and we have seen his glory, the glory as of a father's only son, full of grace and truth" (v. 14).

That's when God finally exhales and changes everything, releasing the Logos into the world like an only child, although not to remain one. Paradoxically, the twofold mission of this only child is to make his Father known and to make more children for him. All who receive the Logos, John says—all who breathe in what God has breathed out—will receive the power to become God's children too.

I know we put all kinds of conditions around that—yes, sure, we're all God's children too, but not like Jesus. He alone is the only. He alone is our clear window into the heart of God. Yet there it is, right on the page: this only child does not love being alone any more than his Father does. He means to enlarge the family, filling the world with more brothers and sisters who are willing to become God's Logos made flesh. He has high expectations of his siblings, too. When it is time for him to go back to where he came from, the Logos will turn to them and say, "'[T]ruly, I tell you, the one who believes in me will also do the works that I do and, in fact, will do greater works than these, because I am going to the Father'" (14:12).

The good news is that this transmission is built into the grand scheme of things, beginning in creation and stretching into the future further than any of us can see. If evolution isn't a bad word for you, you might think of it as divine evolution—the way the Logos keeps coming into the world in different forms at different times, showing us as much of God as we can take in until the next time, when the form may be different but the Logos is the same.

When Jesus goes to the Father, he says, God will send another Comforter to be with them—the Holy Spirit, the Spirit of truth, who will go forth from God as Jesus did. The Spirit will not act the same way Jesus did. It won't have a human body, for one thing (unless you're a fan of *The Shack*), but it too was with God in the beginning, moving over the waters at the genesis of creation—one more life-giving expression of God's energy and purpose.

Christians traditionally draw the line there. The Logos has one name, and that name is Jesus. Along with God the Father and God the Holy Spirit, he completes the Trinity that has been part of baseline Christian belief from the earliest centuries of the church. Yet the same Scripture that informed the Trinity contains intriguing glimpses of other Logos-like energies coming forth from the mouth of God.

In Jewish tradition, Torah is God's energetic word, given to God's people that they might choose life and not death. In one old story, the Torah rested in God's bosom before the creation of the world. Another says that when it came time to start making things, God looked into the Torah the way an architect looks into a blueprint, creating the world for the purpose of revealing the

Torah.[1] Only later did God spell the whole thing out for Moses so he could write it down.

Proverbs 8 introduces another Logos-like energy named Wisdom, sometimes known by her Greek name Sophia. "Ages ago I was set up," she says, "at the first, before the beginning of the earth" (v. 23). When God established the heavens, she was there. "When he marked out the foundations of the earth, then I was beside him, like a master worker," she says, "and I was daily his delight, rejoicing before him always, rejoicing in his inhabited world and delighting in the human race" (vv. 29b–31).

She appears again in the book of Sirach, which was written too late for inclusion in the Jewish Bible, but which shows up in a set of books between the First and Second Testaments in some Christian Bibles. Sirach is approved for use in worship on occasion—as it is today, the second after Christmas Day, when Sophia is on the list of potential speakers along with Jeremiah, Solomon, and John. The preacher gets to choose whose voices will be heard, but as far as I recall I have never heard Lady Wisdom's voice in church. Have you?

If you want to read along, you'll need a Bible with the Apocrypha in it—or the Deuterocanonical books, as they are sometimes called. The book of Sirach comes right after the Wisdom of Solomon and right before the book of Baruch. It might be called Ecclesiasticus in your Bible. If you can't find it now, you can look it up later: Sirach, chapter 24, beginning at the first verse:

> Wisdom praises herself,
>   and tells of her glory in the midst of her people.
> In the assembly of the Most High she opens her mouth,
>   and in the presence of his hosts she tells of her glory:
> "I came forth from the mouth of the Most High,
>   and covered the earth like a mist. I dwelt in the highest heavens,
>   and my throne was in a pillar of cloud.
> Alone I compassed the vault of heaven
>   and traversed the depths of the abyss.
> Over waves of the sea, over all the earth,
>   and over every people and nation I have held sway.

Among all these I sought a resting place;
    in whose territory should I abide?

"Then the Creator of all things gave me a command,
    and my Creator chose the place for my tent.
He said, 'Make your dwelling in Jacob,
    and in Israel receive your inheritance.'
Before the ages, in the beginning, he created me,
    and for all the ages I shall not cease to be.
In the holy tent I ministered before him,
    and so I was established in Zion.
Thus in the beloved city he gave me a resting place,
    and in Jerusalem was my domain.
I took root in an honored people,
    in the portion of the Lord, his heritage. (24:1–12)

Did any of that sound familiar to you? It sounded familiar to me. Wisdom came forth from the mouth of the Most High. She dwelt in the highest heavens, her throne in a pillar of cloud. She could have stayed there, but she wanted a resting place on earth. *How Logos-like of her.* She didn't want to cover the earth like mist anymore; she wanted a zip code, a place to pitch her tent—the same word John used when he said the Logos became flesh and pitched his tent among us. Wisdom wanted to move into the neighborhood, and God was happy to oblige. Looking down at the map, God said, "There." "'Make your dwelling in Jacob, and in Israel receive your inheritance.'" So she took root there, hoping for as many new children as her tent could hold.

It's a pattern you can see over and over again in the sacred story: God's eternal energy for sending the Logos to take up residence in the world, bringing the creation close enough to the creator to be kissed—by Torah, by Wisdom, by Jesus Christ, by Holy Spirit—all of them offering us direct access to the fierce love and creative intelligence that is always looking for a new place to call home. Too often, I think, religious people want to restrict that divine access: the Logos comes only by this name, not that name, to this people only, not that. The last verse of today's Gospel reading certainly sounds like that. "No one has ever seen God," John says in the last line of his prologue. "It is God the only Son, who is close to the Father's heart, who has made him known" (1:18).

What John *doesn't* say is that the only Son is the only one who has ever made God known. Make of that what you will, but I think it's why we need to keep John's Christmas story in the mix. Matthew and Luke have captured our hearts with their stories of Jesus' birth in Bethlehem a long time ago. We can see the baby; we can hear him. The script is familiar, and the costumes have a lot of wear on them. That's part of why we love it: because we know the ropes.

John alone reminds us that the Logos is eternally being born. His story isn't set in the time of King Herod in a town six miles south of Jerusalem. It's set in the cosmos, where the Logos has no beginning or end.

John alone reminds us that the Logos is eternally being born. His story isn't set in the time of King Herod in a town six miles south of Jerusalem. It's set in the cosmos, where the Logos has no beginning or end. This is much more difficult to imagine: that the Logos has been coming into the world forever, spoken by the God whom no one has ever seen, to make the divine energy and purpose known on earth. What kind of costume do you put on that? Is one outfit enough?

During the Christmas season, we recognize the one that is definitive for us—the Logos made Jesus, the Logos made flesh—even as we affirm his coming again in a form we may not recognize next time, and the coming of the Holy Spirit between now and then. The creativity of the Logos is never spent.

One of you is bound to point out Jesus' famous saying in John's Gospel, that "'No one comes to the Father except through me'" (14:6). Yet this is also the Gospel in which he says, "'Whoever believes in me believes not in me but in him who sent me'" (12:44). *What a Logos-like thing to say!* John couldn't see the Sender; no one can. But he couldn't take his eyes off the One the Sender sent, whose story John was given to tell. That made John the Logos for the Logos, the one who got to put his own breath behind God's Word as it landed in his own time and place.

I hate to press the point, but it's your turn now. Jesus said so. Those who believe in him will do the works he did—greater, in fact—now that he has returned to the Source. It is our turn to put our breath behind God's Word so that it lands in our own time and place. However well or poorly things seem to be working out for us, there is something else at work here that has been pouring itself out for us *forever*, which the darkness does not overcome.

Light from light.

Fullness from which we have all received, grace upon grace.

Christmas every day.

Broadcast on *Day 1**
Second Sunday after Christmas Day
January 5, 2020

---

*Day 1 began broadcasting Sunday sermons in 1945 as *The Protestant Hour* and has been on the air every week since, currently on more than two hundred radio stations.

Chapter Seventeen

Mariam the Magnificent

Luke 1:46–49

And Mary said,
"My soul magnifies the Lord,
and my spirit rejoices in God my Savior,
for he has looked with favor on the lowliness of his servant.
Surely, from now on all generations will call me blessed;
for the Mighty One has done great things for me,
and holy is his name."

—Luke 1:46–49

Jesus' mother, Mary, has taken her son's place as our primary teacher today. Part of that is because he has not been born yet, but it is also because God chose her for more reasons than her ability to bear a child. Mary's "yes" was essential to God's purpose. Her willingness to accept the risk that went along with it gave her a place in Christian history like no other. Though we do not often stop to think about it, her wisdom is different from her son's. She has her own perspective on the story, her own way of proclaiming the gospel, which strikes Luke as so important that he makes sure to capture it in the first chapter of his Gospel.

For reasons that are complex and often unsatisfying, Mary is not nearly as important to Protestants as she is to Catholic and

Orthodox Christians. Advent is really the only time she shows up in most Protestant churches, chiefly to hold the baby Jesus in the Christmas pageant and then go back into the closet with Joseph and the shepherds until next year.

Beverly Gaventa, whom some of you know as professor of New Testament at Baylor and a Presbyterian elder, says, "[I]f there is one thing Protestants agree on—across the theological spectrum, women and men, whether in local churches or seminary classrooms—it is that *we* do not talk about Mary."[1] Why is that? "We are the people who do *not* honor Mary and who find such attention threatening to proper Christian devotion to Jesus Christ. We may not know much about Mary, but we know that we do not have anything to do with her."[2]

If Gaventa sounds really certain about this, it is because she has thought, talked, and written about Mary for a long time. Even now, when she is invited to lead continuing education events for clergy or laity, she regularly offers to talk about the role of Mary in Scripture—something Protestants might naturally be interested in, given the high importance they place on the Word of God—but the response she most often receives is, "Oh, I don't think that would attract a very large audience. We're mostly Protestants here."[3]

In her teaching career, Gaventa says, she has probably read at least a hundred student papers on Jesus' exchange with the Syro-Phoenician woman, recorded in two Gospels, but not a single paper on his exchanges with his mother, recorded in all four Gospels—at the Jerusalem Temple, for instance, when she confronts him for losing his family accidentally-on-purpose when he is just twelve years old ("'Child, why have you treated us like this? Look, your father and I have been searching for you in great anxiety'" [Luke 2:48]). Or at a house in the Galilee, where she goes to extract him from his mob of followers and take him home ("'Your mother and your brothers and sisters are outside, asking for you'" [Mark 3:32]). Or at the wedding in Cana of Galilee, when—using her best feminine communication skills—she asks him to produce more wine by saying, "'They have no wine'" (John 2:3), and he sasses her ("'Woman, what concern is that to you and to me? My hour has not yet come'" [2:4]).

Mary not only loves Jesus; she's not afraid of him. She goes toe to toe with him, trying to care for the grown man who is so busy taking care of other people that he won't take care of himself. She is there at the beginning, with no one but poor Joseph for a midwife; and she is there at the end, with one male disciple left to lean on while she listens to her boy give up his last breath. She is there at the garden tomb with the other Mary, and she is there at the new beginning in the upper room, numbered among his disciples.

Mary is easily the most famous woman in the Bible—which leads Gaventa to wonder why the Presbyterian Church's 1991 Brief Statement of Faith lifts up Sarah but makes no mention of Mary at all. "If we speak frankly," she says, "some of us may admit that our response to Mary is a reaction to certain devotional practices that seem excessive."[4] *What, like Protestants are innocent of excessive devotional practices?*

On your behalf, I researched the Jesus toaster, manufactured by a company called Burnt Impressions, which scorches Jesus' image onto slices of bread. In the process, I discovered the Evangecube, a seven-picture cube that "simply and clearly unfolds the gospel of Jesus Christ" for use on mission trips and church outreach events. Don't get me started on the excessive devotional practices of some Protestants I know.

Gaventa goes on to make her central point: that if Protestants are going to talk about Mary—if they are going to give her a second chance to resume her rightful place in the Christian story—then they are going to have to do it in a Protestant-like way. This will mean finding her in Scripture, listening both to what Scripture says *about* her as well as what Scripture allows her to say for herself. "To raise only the most obvious question," Gaventa concludes, "what would it mean for Protestants to take seriously the words of Mary" in the Magnificat, that "'All generations will call me blessed'"?[5]

The plot thickens here, since there are so many scriptural views of Mary from which to choose. Is it the timid teenager who is blessed, the one who accepts Gabriel's proposal when he comes on God's behalf to ask for her hand? *Let it be with me according to your word.* Or is it the unmarried mother-to-be who is blessed, the one who is so caught up in what God is bringing into the world through her body that she has no time for shame? *For the Mighty One has done great things for me, and holy is his name.* Is Mary blessed because she is so quiet or because she is so outspoken—because she is such a good mother or because she is such a good prophet?

You can say "all of the above" if you want but based on every Christmas pageant I have ever seen, the church has cast its vote for the quiet Mary—the acquiescent one, whose chief virtue is her ability to bear a son. I hear that Trinity Presbyterian Church's preschoolers are putting on their pageant this morning, and I love the fact that you place no limit on how many Josephs or Marys there can be. If they're called, they're called!

I haven't seen the script you use here, but I looked up a couple of free ones online to refresh my memory, and sure enough: all Mary does is sit there. Prophets and angels have lots of lines; shepherds and magi have lots of lines. Even Gabriel has lots of lines, but Mary has only one line: "I will happily carry out God's will," she says. (Stage direction: "Mary looks toward heaven with a smile on her face.")[6]

There's no hope this will ever happen, but I wish we could hear Matthew's story one year (prophets and magi!) and Luke's story the next (angels and shepherds!) so that Mary got to say more at least every other year. Luke's her advocate, after all—the evangelist who tells the whole story of Jesus' birth through her eyes, not Joseph's. Luke's also the one who spells her name in Greek as Mariam, not Marias, saying something important about her that Matthew never does.

Mary, Marias, Mariam, Miriam—what's the difference? The difference is that Miriam is a Hebrew name. It was one of the most popular names for a Jewish girl in first-century Palestine, not because it was the name of Jesus' mother but because it was the name of Moses' sister: the brave young Miriam who saved her baby brother's life by putting him up for adoption where Pharaoh's daughter was sure to find him (Exod. 2:3); the prophet Miriam, who banged her tambourine and sang a victory song when the

Israelites arrived on the safe side of the Red Sea (15:20–21); the insubordinate Miriam, who joined her brother Aaron in questioning Moses' authority by asking, "'Has the LORD spoken only through Moses? Has he not spoken through us also?'" (Num. 12:2).

The fact that every single English translation of Luke renders this name "Mary" instead of "Mariam" tells you as much as the Christmas pageant does. This Mary has no history, no ancestors in the faith. She has come into the world to bear Jesus, and her womb is the most important thing about her—that, and her willingness to say, "I will happily carry out God's will" before turning her face toward heaven. She enters history as the mother of the Christ. By extension, she is the mother of all Christians.

Mariam, on the other hand, has a much longer memory. She is the Jewish girl who has the chutzpah to question the angel Gabriel when he presents her with God's plan ("'How can this be, since I am a virgin?'" [Luke 1:34]). She is the pregnant, unwed young woman who goes missing from her family to visit her cousin Elisheva, whose own miracle baby does a flip inside her when she opens the door to Mariam. "'Blessed are you among women,'" Elisheva says, "'and blessed is the fruit of your womb'" (v. 42).

That's when Mariam lets loose the Magnificat, Luke says—singing her heart out like her namesake did on the far side of her own Red Sea—about God's defense of the defenseless, God's rescue of the lowly, God's upheaval of the proud and overthrow of those in power. It's a good thing none of Herod's people can hear this Mariam's song, because they know what to do with people like her. But this Mariam is fearless in her praise of God's faithfulness to the old, old promise—not a promise that will be *replaced* by the child Mariam is about to bear but one that will be *renewed* in the flesh of this unlikely mother and her unlikely child.

Whatever is about to happen, she knows it's going down in history—the first chapter for someone named Mary, perhaps, but not for someone named Mariam. For someone named Mariam, the God of old is already thousands and thousands of pages deep into the story of salvation, as committed as ever to those made in the divine image, for whom God is about to do a new thing as startling as the things God has done before.

For someone named Mariam, the God of old is already thousands and thousands of pages deep into the story of salvation, as committed as ever to those made in the divine image, for whom God is about to do a new thing as startling as the things God has done before.

Watch this, God says, sending an extremely competent angel named Gabriel to visit a very formidable Jewish girl named Mariam in a backwater town in north central Galilee. Depending on what she says (all you can do is ask), her answer could be the best verse yet in the song God has been singing since Sinai: "'I will walk among you and be your God, and you will be my people'" (Lev. 26:12 NIV).

It's all in the Bible. There are no rosaries or religious statues required, but wouldn't it be wonderful if we could get the Magnificat back into the Christmas pageant, so our children grow up knowing Mariam the prophet as well as Mary the mother mild? If we gave her a tambourine, I am pretty sure the kids would never forget her. They might even have some context for the things we tell them later about her son, raised by a mother who knew all about the cost of breaking rules, bearing insults, making dangerous speeches, and ascribing it all to God. You *know* he got his cheekbones from her, or at least the color of his eyes. (Where else would he have gotten them?) Why not her *valor* as well?

"'All generations will call me blessed.'" It's true! Now you get to decide *why*.

Trinity Presbyterian Church,
Atlanta, Georgia
Third Sunday of Advent
December 14, 2014

Chapter Eighteen

Time to Face the Demons

Luke 9:37–43

Just then a man from the crowd shouted, "Teacher, I beg you to look at my son; he is my only child. Suddenly a spirit seizes him, and all at once he shrieks. It convulses him until he foams at the mouth; it mauls him and will scarcely leave him. I begged your disciples to cast it out, but they could not."

—Luke 9:38–40

If tomorrow is Fat Tuesday—the day we're supposed to eat enough sweets and drink enough silliness to get it all out of our systems before Lent—then today is Sober Monday, a day to consider that the forty days ahead of us may not be about giving up chocolate, scotch, or television (television! Jesus never said one bad word about television!). Instead, the days to come are about sitting quietly in the wilderness, without all our usual distractions, to remember what is saving our lives now. If we can do that, then we'll have a better chance of facing the demons when they come, creeping out from behind the rocks where we can see them after the sun goes down.

Wilderness is a frame of mind as well as a landscape. You can enter the wilderness simply by sitting down somewhere without a book, a phone, or set of headphones, and telling God you're ready. You can enter the wilderness by boxing up all your pacifiers for a few weeks, declining to fill any more of the white spaces on your calendars, stopping whatever it is that you do to keep yourself too occupied for God to get to you, and declaring yourself ready to encounter God in any way God chooses.

I don't know what you use to keep yourself from feeling what you're really feeling, but *you* do. When you scroll down the list of possible sedatives and come to the one that you have a physical reaction to giving up, then you're probably on the wilderness runway. I discovered one that made me flinch lately, in a book by Lauren Winner called *Girl Meets God*. If you know the book, then I hope you'll grant me literary license, since I am telling this story from memory.

Winner was a new Christian when she decided to practice Lent in earnest for the first time. She wanted to choose the perfect thing to give up, so she sat down in her apartment to think about it. The place was more or less furnished with books—books lining the walls, books on the windowsills, books stacked beside her bed, on the table where she ate, by her favorite chair. She never went anywhere without a book, she said. She always had one with her, so that if she ever found herself with a moment to spare, she could whip that baby out and read a few pages.

I don't remember the first thing she decided to give up for Lent because it didn't stick. When she met with her priest to tell him whatever it was, he let her sit there for a minute. Then he asked if she might consider giving up reading instead. *Give up reading for six weeks?!* I had a physical reaction to that, both when he suggested it and when she decided to do it. The list of reasons why I could never do it went on and on, until I got to the one that was buried way down at the bottom of the list because it clearly had the most power over me: reading was my escape hatch. It was how I took my mind off things I didn't want to think about. It was better than a pill, better than a drink, better than a Netflix miniseries at getting me out of my problems and into someone else's.

Reading may not be your thing, but you do have a thing—maybe even a very good thing—that keeps you out of the wilderness so you don't have to face the beasts. Even if you're not ready to give your thing up, not even for a little while, it helps to know its name. On Sober Monday, you can at least circle it and wonder how it came to have so much power over you.

It also helps to remember that while the wilderness may be a scary place, that doesn't automatically make it a bad place. Biblically speaking, it's a holy place—one of the most reliable places where people of faith can be sure to encounter God. The people of Israel spent forty years in the wilderness, learning to live without pacifiers. The prophet Elijah spent forty days in the wilderness before he heard the voice of God in the sound of sheer silence. Jesus went into the wilderness following his baptism (actually, the Gospel of Mark says the Spirit *drove* him there). Paul went there after his vision on the road to Damascus. The wilderness is a time-honored place for sorting things out, for giving up beloved distractions, for deciding to live on one day's manna at a time instead of a camper full of the comforts of home.

Civilization offers so many things that promise to save us— heart-healthy food, wise investments, three-ton SUVs jam-packed with air bags. When we bite, it's because we're doing our best to stay alive, both for ourselves and for our children. We want to make the most of the gift that has been given us, but I'll tell you what: if you're not careful, those lifesavers can fool you. They can start out looking like saviors and end up acting like little demons that possess you instead of you possessing them. They can cost more life than they give.

That's why the church has long recommended an annual sab-batical in the wilderness—forty days of living in a different way, crossways to a culture that insists you cannot live without all of its expensive safety features. For forty days, you get to survive on simple manna suppers. For forty days, you get to enter the tent of meeting with God, so that you are better equipped to out your demons. If you don't get scared, then it's not working, but do not lose heart. It is not until you have encountered the Really Real, after all, that you can tell the difference between that and all the lesser gods who try to pass for real.

We want to make the most of the gift that has been given us, but I'll tell you what: if you're not careful, those lifesavers can fool you. They can start out looking like saviors and end up acting like little demons that possess you instead of you possessing them. They can cost more life than they give.

Here is the subtle genius of Luke's storytelling. We don't come cold to today's story about the demon-possessed boy. We come from the mountain of the transfiguration where we, along with Peter, James, and John, have just gotten a full dose of God's spooky, liberating glory. Having encountered the Really Real—both in the divine cloud and in the divine son to whom God has commanded us to listen—we are better equipped to recognize the unholy spirit that is making this poor boy unrecognizable to his own father.

According to Luke, the demon-possessed boy is also an only son. "'Teacher, I beg you to look at my son,'" the father says. "'He is my only child.'" Thus we have two only sons operating under the influence of two different spirits—one spirit in the lifesaving business and the other spirit in the bondage business. Bringing them face-to-face like this, right after what has happened on the mountain, Luke expects us to be able to tell the spirits apart. He also expects us to know which one is more Real.

Compared to other exorcists of his time—and there were plenty—Jesus of Nazareth was a minimalist. When he dealt with demons, he did not make use of charms or amulets. He did not cast spells or go into a trance. He did not lean over the body of the possessed person and make strange sounds while he did things that he made sure no one else could see. He simply commanded the unclean spirits to get lost and they did—sometimes quietly, sometimes spectacularly—but still, the unclean spirits did what Jesus told them to do. In the reality of his presence, their so-called reality was exposed for what it was: parasitic, dependent, *over*. A word from him was all it took to send them packing.

In the present case, Jesus was not the first person the father asked to free his child from the unclean spirit. "'I begged your disciples to cast it out,'" the father says, "'but they could not.'" This infuriates Jesus, who blasts everyone in hearing distance. "'You faithless and perverse generation,'" he says. "'How much longer must I be with you and bear with you?'" (v. 41).

If you can stand the blast, there's actually something pretty wonderful in it. Jesus apparently thinks his disciples *should* be able to do this work. Those who have encountered the Really Real—whose shining has rubbed off on them—should not be flummoxed by a simple convulsing demon.

Once, when a friend of mine came out of his prayers laughing, I said, "What's so funny?"

"What God just said," he said.

"That was funny?" I said.

"Yeah," he said. "I was just doing my usual begging, asking God to make me a better person, to look after Gran, to help Stephen through his surgery, when these words came into my head, clear as anything."

"What words?" I said.

"Well, I think God just said: 'Don't ask me to do anything you can do for yourself.'"

Or, to paraphrase Luke, "You trustless deviants! Am I the only exorcist around here? Bring your son here." Then Jesus rebuked the unclean spirit, healed the boy, and gave him back to his father. "And all were astounded at the greatness of God" (v. 43).

Of course, we do not believe in demons anymore. We have other words to explain why a young boy like this might have had convulsions and foamed at the mouth. The poor kid was probably suffering from epilepsy or some kind of dissociative disorder. Tourette's syndrome? He may even have had a brain tumor. He didn't need an exorcist. He needed a good neurological consult and a treatment plan.

Maybe, but to read this story scientifically strikes me as profoundly *unimaginative*. We may not call them demons anymore, but I know plenty of unholy spirits that steal into people and rob them of their freedom.

I know the spirit that makes people eat what will not nourish them and buy what they cannot afford by convincing them that these things will fulfill them, when all that is filled are the pockets of those who care nothing about them but how much they can consume.

I know the spirit that makes people work longer and longer hours at jobs that never get done by persuading them that terrible things will happen to them and those they love if they don't make enough bricks to see them through a menacing future.

I know the spirit that makes people more and more afraid of each other by telling them that the demons are all out there—banging on our doors, trying to take what is ours—and that anyone who believes differently is clearly working for the other side.

I know the spirit that makes people believe they deserve the terrible things that have happened to them by persuading them that God is an angry father with righteous fists, whose punishments are for their own good.

If we aren't all rolling around on the ground foaming at the mouth, maybe that's because we have learned to live too well with the unclean spirits that possess us. Plenty of us don't even recognize their presence anymore, including those of us with symptoms. All we know is that we can't sleep at night, that we live at the edge of tears, that we lash out in ways that aren't like us, which is actually a hopeful sign since it means that we still have some sense of what we *are* really like, even when we do not seem free to act from that God-given center.

The good news this Sober Monday is that we know an exorcist—someone whose reality is so strong, because his intimacy with the Really Real is so great—who is capable of rebuking the unholy spirits. He is capable of restoring us to our senses so we can choose our own lives again, once we are free from the imposters who will never stop trying to take God's place. He even thinks we can do this work, at least if we work together. *Don't ask me to do anything you can do for yourselves.*

If you were hoping to get by with giving up chocolate or scotch this Lent, then by all means start there. Just don't stop there, at least not if it's real life you want. If real life is what you want, then spend enough time in the wilderness to face the real demons. You might be surprised to find that some of them need your blessing, not your rebuke. Either way, you have nothing finally to fear from them. God is great, you know what is Real, and you have a Savior near at hand. One word from him is all it takes.

First Presbyterian Church,
Greensboro, North Carolina
Monday before Ash Wednesday
February 19, 2007

Chapter Nineteen

The Wake-Up Call

Luke 13:1–9

At that very time there were some present who told him about the Galileans whose blood Pilate had mingled with their sacrifices. He asked them, "Do you think that because these Galileans suffered in this way they were worse sinners than all other Galileans? No, I tell you; but unless you repent, you will all perish as they did."
—Luke 13:1–3

I love Episcopalians. We're so well trained that we'll say, "Praise to you, Lord Christ," after *anything*, including that prickly pear of a Gospel we just heard. Dead Galileans, bloody sacrifices, falling towers, hatchet-happy vineyard owners. *Praise to you, Lord Christ.*

We can talk about it later, but I think this is the church's way of training us in faith. By asking us to praise Christ no matter what while we are *in here*, the church hopes we will learn to praise Christ no matter what when we are back *out there*. By responding the same way no matter what, we learn to separate our present likes and dislikes, our clear comforts and discomforts, from our trust that God is present in them all. Good health and good friends under sunny skies? *Praise to you, Lord Christ.* Scared to death, with no idea what will happen next? *Praise to you, Lord Christ.* It is a trust exercise—one that we repeat over and over again because none of us is any good at it. Day by day, most of us reserve our praise for the good news, not the bad news. We even like to think we can affect what kind of news we get by being good ourselves.

This morning's Gospel begins with a crowd of people who have received some very bad news. The Roman governor, Pontius Pilate, has apparently slaughtered some rebel Galileans, mingling their blood with the blood of their sacrifices to God. That they were killed in the act of worship strikes those present as particularly awful—as awful as people being gunned down in church on a Sunday morning right in the middle of Communion. What was God thinking? What could it possibly mean?

Based on Jesus' response to the crowd, they think it means God was punishing those people for their sins. I think I actually heard something like that from a Christian evangelist after a recent earthquake hit Haiti. What did he say? That the Haitians had "made a pact to the devil" during their revolution, promising to serve the devil if he would free them from the French. The devil said, "OK, it's a deal," the evangelist said, and "they have been cursed by one thing after the other" ever since.[1]

It's a convenient explanation of why things happen the way they do. If you assert that there's a direct connection between the bad things that happen to people and the badness of the people themselves, then all you have to do is be less bad than they are and hope God stays busy with them. Figure out where the red zone is so you can stay out of it. Decide how much you can disappoint God without being cut down so you can stop just short of that.

But the spiritual accountants in today's story get nowhere with Jesus. Give it up, he tells them. The ones who died weren't any worse than some of you, but God's mind doesn't work the way yours does. While you're trying to figure out how much you can get away with and still hang on to your life the way it is, God is dying for you to want more than that. God never stops offering you a way of life that runs at a right angle from the one you are living, and if you don't turn in that direction pretty soon then you're going to be a ghost whether a building falls on you or not.

God won't have to do a thing to you. You'll do it to yourself, by persisting in your barren, your accidental lives.

Then Jesus tells them the parable of the Fig Tree, which is not the version most of us know best. Mark and Matthew tell the more familiar story—the one that comes from the last week of Jesus' life, when he was so hungry—for some way out, for some sign that anyone understood one word that he was saying, for some relief from the gnawing inside of him—that he walked over to a fig tree in leaf and reached his hand into it for something to eat. He reached left and right. He reached high and low, but no matter where he reached, his hand closed on nothing but leaves. So he cursed the fig tree—the only thing he ever cursed in his whole life—and it withered right there in front of him.

If Luke knew that story, he left it out of his Gospel. Maybe he didn't believe in a Jesus who would do something like that, especially when it wasn't even the season for figs. Maybe he was covering up for a messiah who acted for one moment like an ordinary man, lashing out at a disappointing world with all judgment and no grace. Whatever his reason, Luke left that story out, substituting another story about another fig tree that does not show up in any of the other Gospels.

It is not a story told *about* Jesus but a story told *by* him on his way to Jerusalem—a teaching story he offers to the same crowd that thinks God punishes people for their sins by dropping buildings on them. The parable starts out the same way the familiar fig tree story does: a man comes looking for fruit and finds none. This is not a stray fig tree growing by the side of the road, however. This is the man's own tree, planted in his vineyard, where it has been sucking up everything it needs to live without giving anything back for years now.

Every year the man reaches into his tree and every year he finds nothing. He reaches left and right. He reaches high and low. But no matter where he reaches, his hand closes on nothing but leaves. The man knows what this means: less sweetness in the world. No fig jam, no fig tarts, no figs. Meanwhile, the tree has grown so bushy that it is putting some of the grapevines in the shade. The ones nearest the fig tree are looking distinctly puny, with leaves that are smaller and paler than those on vines that are farther away. It is past time for the tree to go, not because it is *bad* but because it is supposed to be *good*. It is supposed to bear figs—that is its purpose in the world—but instead of figs it is producing nothing but shade. So the man orders his gardener to cut the tree down.

The owner is clearly a member of John the Baptist's church, where every tree that does not bear good fruit is cut down and thrown into the fire. But his gardener must belong to some other church, because he pleads for the tree's life. "Let it alone," he says—or, in his own tongue, "forgive it," as in "forgive them, for they know not what they do." Give me one more year with it, the gardener says to his boss, then you can cut it down and I won't stand in your way.

The gardener is pleading with the vineyard owner, but he is also defying him. Did you hear that? "*You* can cut it down." I won't do it, not even then, but if you still insist on killing it a year from now then *you* can cut it down.

If you staged this parable, I think you'd need three players, not two: (1) a vineyard owner with every right to cut down a fruitless tree, (2) a defiant gardener willing to work to save the tree, and (3) a very anxious tree, shifting from root to root while it waits to discover what will become of it.

People who cannot stand the tension in the story turn it into an allegory, featuring God as the hatchet-happy vineyard owner and Jesus as the tender gardener standing between the ax and us. I have even heard a couple of preachers use this story to contrast the Old Testament God of judgment with the New Testament God of grace, which effectively turns God into an anti-Semite with a multiple personality disorder.

Jesus is a much better storyteller than that. He lets the parable do its work by leaving it loose. He doesn't even finish it. He just lets us listen to the conversation between the vineyard owner and the gardener—the same way the fig tree does—trusting us to find the gospel in it.

Since parables are do-it-yourselfers, the gospel I find may not
be the gospel you find, but my point of view is definitely that of
the tree. I spend a lot of my life pushing out leaves and branches,
figuring there is still time to concentrate on the fruit. The leaves
and branches are not inconsequential. They include keeping my
house in good order, paying bills on time, meeting all kinds of
deadlines, sending cards to sick friends, staying on top of email,
working out twice a week, and remembering to vote. The problem is that none of those things is what I was put on earth to
do—the fruit part. I need time to think about that, time to make
the kinds of changes that will allow it to flourish. So the fruit part
keeps getting moved from "now" to "eventually."

Jesus is a much better storyteller than that. He lets the
parable do its work by leaving it loose. He doesn't even
finish it. He just lets us listen to the conversation between
the vineyard owner and the gardener—the same way the
fig tree does—trusting us to find the gospel in it.

Do you know what I mean? Jesus' story isn't meant to induce
guilt. It's meant to wake us up, since it is so much easier to stay
semiconscious—driving along expecting everyone to stay in their
own lanes, convincing ourselves that the people stopped on the
shoulders with blue lights flashing are there because they have
done something wrong, that if we just keep our insurance up to
date and our eyes on the road, then we will get where we are
going in plenty of time tonight and can put off thinking about
what really matters for a less stressful day.

Then the car ahead of you slams on its brakes and you do it too,
though not in time to avoid crashing into it. The truck behind
you does the same thing, until all three of you are sitting there in
your crushed cars with the traffic whizzing by, amazed to be alive.

Or maybe it's your doctor who wakes you up, calling first thing in
the morning after your annual physical to ask if you are sitting down.

Or maybe it's the picture in the newspaper of an eighteen-year-old soldier saying good-bye to her father before she ships overseas. For just a minute, you are inside her skin—five feet tall, in your Army uniform, with your senior prom just ten months behind you—your daddy's hands on your shoulders, the back of your mouth full of tears, your two duffel bags in the back of your family's van. God did not drop this building on you, but it happened. Now what?

As awful as it sounds, I think nothing is more clarifying than the reminder of the ax near all our roots—not because an angry God put it there but because the grass withers, the flower fades, and none of us by worrying can add a single hour to our span of life. That is a message so hard for most of us to get that it takes something really dramatic to get our attention long enough to wonder if we are living our real lives—the ones we were put on this earth to live—and if not, if there is still time. Is it too late to do the things that matter, to love the people who have been waiting to be loved, to seek the God who wills to be found?

I am convinced that the longing to bear fruit—to live lives that matter—is embedded in us as deeply as the longing to eat, sleep, love, and be loved. The problem is that such lives don't happen automatically. They require a certain alertness to the way things really are, both in us and in the world; a certain willingness to make choices we would not make if we thought time would never run out; a certain awareness that we need all the help we can get, from any gardener willing to tend our roots. Today's Gospel teaching is given to us to remember why we are here—but what if we don't get around to it? What if the car crashes before we get where we are going? What if the diagnosis is terminal, or the young soldier is killed on her first tour of duty?

God does not drop buildings on people. Jesus said so. But time really does run out.

Whether our lives are cut short or we live until our branches grow moss on them, no one lives forever. And God knows the world needs fruit as much as we need to produce it.

The good news is that we do not know how today's story ends. The owner makes his case. The gardener makes his. The story ends with the fig tree still alive—never *more* alive—with maybe as much as a whole year to put more sweetness in this world.

Praise to you, Lord Christ, for sunlight and manure, for pruning shears and the solidity of the ax. Praise to you the vineyard owner and to you the gardener—but where is the Holy Spirit in this parable? I am glad you asked. Praise to the she-bird sitting on her nest deep in the branches of the fig tree, enjoying the breeze, the view, and all those lovely green *leaves*.

Trinity Episcopal Church,*
Boston, Massachusetts
Second Sunday in Lent
February 28, 2010

---

*An earlier version of this sermon was given at Saint Charles Avenue Baptist Church in New Orleans in 2001.

Chapter Twenty

Bathing Deep

John 13:1–9

And during supper Jesus, knowing that the Father had given all things into his hands, and that he had come from God and was going to God, got up from the table, took off his outer robe, and tied a towel around himself. Then he poured water into a basin and began to wash the disciples' feet and to wipe them with the towel that was tied around him.

—John 13:2b–5

Before I begin, let me ask for a show of hands. How many of you have *ever* taken part in a footwashing ceremony at a church? Okay, now how many of you go to churches that offer footwashing once a year during Holy Week, usually on Maundy Thursday? Last question: How many of you belong to churches where you wash feet on a regular basis, at least as often as you share the Lord's Supper?

Just as I suspected! On that last question, not a single hand in the air. But why? In John's Gospel, where there is no mention of Jesus passing around bread and wine on the night before he died, there is clear mention of him washing their feet, and instructing them to follow his example by doing it for one another when he is gone.

After Jesus has finished washing at least twenty-four separate feet—not just Peter's but also Judas' and everyone else's—after he has untied the wet towel from around his waist, put his robe back on, and returned to the table, he looks around at his friends and says,

"Do you know what I have done to you? You call me Teacher and Lord—and you are right, for that is what I am. So if I, your Lord and Teacher, have washed your feet, you also ought to wash one another's feet. For I have set you an example, that you also should do as I have done to you." (vv. 12b–15)

Yet the majority of Christians don't, or at least don't very often, which makes footwashing the neglected sacrament, the one that failed to capture the imagination of the early church and the one still ignored by most mainline Christians today.

The Church of the Brethren still practices it regularly, along with some Mennonites, Baptists, and Pentecostals, but even in churches that claim seven sacraments (like mine) footwashing is not one of them. Episcopalians seem vaguely embarrassed by the whole thing—the suds, the spills, the wonky toes, the yellowed toenails. Even once a year seems a bit *much*, don't you think? Surely once in a *lifetime* would fulfill the Lord's command while sparing his followers all that *mess*.

A couple of years ago I co-taught a class on Christian practice at a seminary with another minister named Liz. Forty people showed up for four days of talking about the ways we learn faith by what we do in our bodies—not just the obvious things like taking part in baptism, Communion, and the laying on of hands, but also the less obvious things like singing hymns, visiting the sick, going on pilgrimage, and walking a labyrinth.

After the whole group had talked and talked about these things for days and days, Liz and I decided to wrap up the week by *doing* something instead of *talking* about it. A wordless footwashing was the obvious choice: no talking, just washing, with full confidence that the act itself would teach us what we needed to know.

When Liz and I started planning how we would do it, I suggested that we just surprise everybody, the same way Jesus surprised his disciples in John's Gospel. No one knew what Jesus was going to do that last night. He had not given them advance notice, so they could be sure not to wear panty hose or trim their toenails. I suggested we do the same thing with the people in our class, so they could actually feel Peter's recoil—*Oh no you don't; you're not washing my feet.*

Liz wisely pointed out that neither of us was Jesus and that footwashing was not a commonplace practice in our world the way it was in his. She proposed that we tell people what we were going to do ahead of time, adding an alternative of hand anointing for those who were timid about their feet. We even made provision for people who did not want anyone touching their hands *or* their feet. "The only requirement is that you stay in the room," we told the class. "You may nap, you may pray, or you may watch. All we ask is that you stay in the room."

The minute we announced these plans, class members went into full revolt. They said they appreciated our emphasis on actual practice, but what they really wanted was more history, more theology, more books they could read on what we had been talking about for four days. They said they wanted us to use our last session discussing the stimulating concepts we had introduced. They said they had a few more questions to ask. *Please, please, can't we stay in our heads? We'll do anything! Just don't make us touch each other!*

One woman said that rituals like footwashing were hollow shells left over from the Middle Ages and that she was seeking a ritual-free approach to God. I forget whether she was a happy Quaker or an angry Catholic, but she could have run for mayor of that class and gotten elected on the first ballot.

Tom Driver, who for many years taught at Union Seminary in New York, once observed that spirit-filled acts like footwashing fall on hard times in churches that put high value on social respectability. They "shy away from experiences that are strongly anti-structural," he said, "preferring the shelter of this world's customs even in ritual."[1]

I know he's right, but it's an odd thing to say when you consider how vital water is to human existence. Scripture is full of it—from the waters of creation in the book of Genesis to the river flowing from the throne of God in the book of Revelation. Jesus was baptized in it. He drank from deep wells of it. He washed his disciples' feet in it and told them to do likewise. Since when did bathing a body part become "strongly anti-structural"?

One woman said that rituals like footwashing were hollow shells left over from the Middle Ages and that she was seeking a ritual-free approach to God. I forget whether she was a happy Quaker or an angry Catholic, but she could have run for mayor of that class and gotten elected on the first ballot.

Even if you're a shower person, you know how bathing can turn the hottest day on record into one that may be bearable. It can convince your sore muscles that there may really be a tomorrow, or simply turn you back into someone your loved ones want to be around. Maybe it's the way a bath signals the end of the workday, or the beginning of the weekend. Maybe it's the way a bath allows us to touch ourselves tenderly, bringing us back to the naked truth of our bodies with all their wonders and vulnerability.

Or maybe it's the way a bath awakens our deep memory of where we came from, growing in private oceans inside our mother's bodies, breathing water instead of air. That first bath not only gave us what we needed to grow; it also cushioned us from blows, allowed us to move more easily, and kept the temperature steady while recycling our fluids as well as any space station. Every mother I know can tell you where she was when her water broke, just as a father can remember the first time he bathed his child in a plastic basin or a kitchen sink, dipping a cloth in warm soapy water and running it over his baby's skin.

Of course, plenty of us remember bathing people at the other end of life too—perhaps warily at first, having arrived at such intimacy with no real training or warning, but then gradually forgetting what all the formality was about. It's just a bath, right? Finally, we become as familiar with someone else's ailing body as we are with our own. A warm washcloth at the corners of the eyes is hard to beat. So is having each finger tugged through a hot towel so that the smell of eucalyptus stays on the skin.

Biblically speaking, a bath has no fixed meaning. Scriptural baths are sensuous, healing, judging, restoring. People bathe to be cleansed from dirt and sin, to be made whole and holy again, to become more attractive to a potential suitor. People bathe in water, blood, milk, and dew. They bathe in rivers, pools, springs, and tubs. They are bathed in birth and they are bathed again in death. What this means, among other things, is that water cannot be tamed, not even by putting it in a basin. Even there, it rises up from the deeps and carries us back to the deeps with no permission from us to do so, simply by being what it is.

At that class I was telling you about, Liz and I quelled the rebellion. The Christians agreed to at least stay in the room for the strongly anti-structural experience coming up. *Whew.* I knew there were some clergy who would participate to set a good example, and some eldest children who would go through with it whether they wanted to or not, but it was still a toss-up how many people would actually get wet.

"Unless I wash you, you have no share with me" (v. 8). That saying of Jesus didn't faze them a bit.

Liz did her best to improve the odds by turning the chapel into a sacred spa. When I walked in, all the chairs were arranged in a huge circle around the Communion table, except for four pairs of chairs facing one another with empty basins and pitchers of water on the floor in between. None of the containers matched. There was a ceramic pasta bowl, an enamel washbasin with flowers painted on it, a clear glass pitcher, a copper plant waterer. Thank God for Liz! I would have gone straight to Target and bought matching pairs of everything, but Liz knew it was important to use old things, familiar things, the kinds of things people might find in their own homes and kitchens. Who knew? Even if this sacrament never caught on in church, it might still catch on in people's houses, where almost no one had sterling silver basins or embroidered towels set aside for the purpose.

On the Communion table, a dozen flames were flickering—short fat candles, tall skinny ones, candles in glass holders, and candles on brass candlesticks. The smell of vanilla and fresh linen filled the air. The table also held several kinds of scented oil in bottles and jars. That's where the vanilla smell was coming from, along with layers of ginger, fig, and cedar. Piles of clean towels were stacked in front of the table.

Liz and I had planned to give lots of instructions at the beginning of the service to calm people down. We were going to read Scripture to underscore the fact that what we were doing was *biblical.* Then we were going to say a prayer and begin. But after everyone was in place, I watched Liz change her mind. She looked around at each one of us, smiling and taking her time. Then she said, "Everything is here. There is no right way to do this, which means you can't do it wrong. The Spirit is here. All are invited to come."

And they did. Slowly at first, then more and more, until people had to fetch chairs from other parts of the room so that they could wash one another's feet and anoint one another's hands, saying everything they needed to say without saying a single word.

After I had my hands rubbed with ginger lotion by a woman the same age as my mother, I went back to my chair and watched people bathe each other: two men who had sat next to one another all week without touching; a woman whose grown son had killed himself the previous summer, washing the feet of another woman who had told us about being sexually abused as a child.

Finally, I focused on a married couple who had been fighting on and off all week—quietly, but you could still tell there was something going on with them that was taking more out of them than usual. The woman went first, removing her husband's shoes and socks as if he were one of their own children. Then she placed his right foot in the glass basin, poured warm water over it, took a bar of white soap in her hands, and started working up a lather.

When she took his foot in her hands, she did it with such tenderness that he began to weep, bending over her as far as he could without falling off his chair. As soon as she realized what was happening above her she started crying too, until I actually watched a woman bathing a man's foot with her tears.

When she was through, he put his arms under hers and helped her to a chair. Then he knelt in front of her and took all the rings off her hands. The wedding ring took some doing, but he finally got it off. Then he anointed her hands, taking each of her small ones in his big ones and kneading them until they were soft. Then he lifted her hands to his wet face, placing one on each side and holding them there: his hands on her hands on his face.

They stayed that way for a while, just letting the water work. Then he took her left hand in his, fished around on the floor for her wedding ring, and put it back on her finger. It slid right on this time. That's when I looked away, remembering that three is a crowd.

When it was all over no one had anything much to say. We circled up, blessed one another, and said good-bye. Class was dismissed. I walked out of the chapel behind the "rituals-are-hollow-shells" woman, who was apologizing to her companion.

"Wow," she said, wiping the snot from her nose, "I can't believe what I said about rituals before."

I don't know if Jesus was inventing a ritual that last night when he washed the feet of his friends, but I believe he was showing them how they could get really, really close to him whenever they missed him too much, or lost their ways, or wondered what they should do next. "For I have set you an example," he said to them when he was finished, "that you also should do as I have done to you."

It is one of those things you don't have to understand to do. All you need is one other person, a bowl, a towel, and some water. Bend over it for any reason at all—to cleanse, to heal, to refresh, to forgive—and you too can hear the wind of God sweeping over the face of the waters. For this is how life begins, again and again and again, wherever two or three are willing to get wet.

The Chautauqua Institution,
Chautauqua, New York
July 19, 2012

Chapter Twenty-One

Follow the Bread

John 21:1–17

*Jesus said to them, "Come and have breakfast." Now none of the
disciples dared to ask him, "Who are you?" because they knew it was
the Lord. Jesus came and took the bread and gave it to them, and
did the same with the fish.*

—John 21:12–13

Follow the money, people say when they are trying to get to the
bottom of something corrupt. Follow the money and it will lead
you to the perp. Since they are so often right, I want to take the
advice but change the subject. It is bread I want to follow today—
not to the perp, but to God. Follow the bread and it will lead you
to the source of all life. That is John's Gospel in a sentence, but
the bread in it is not for believers only. It is bread for the world—
the one God so loves—and for everyone in it whose stomach has
ever growled.

The story of Jesus' breakfast on the beach with his disciples is
rich with earthy detail: a boat full of fishermen who have been up
all night for nothing, watching day break on the surface of the
water because they are too tired to raise their heads to the sky;
a mysterious stranger on the beach, yelling instructions to them
across the water; then a sudden churning of the water on one side

of the boat, with so many fish shoving into the net that the disciples have to scramble to weigh down the other side.

Then a light bulb comes on over Simon Peter's head. When scarcity turns to abundance, who is usually there? Thinking he knows who is doing the yelling, Peter leaps up and *puts on some clothes* so he can jump into the sea ("for he was naked," the text says [v. 7]), leaving the others to do the heavy lifting while he acts on the first impulse that comes into his head. For those of you who know Peter, this sounds just like him.

The scene that follows has something for all five of the senses: charcoal fire for the cold skin, cook smoke for the nose, Jesus for the eyes and ears, fish and bread for the mouth. It is a scene that speaks to the body, which is all the more remarkable since this is a resurrection appearance—the third time Jesus has appeared to his disciples after his death, John says, for those who are counting.

What is notable for our purposes is that he does not come back as a see-through spirit, with disembodied wisdom to share with his friends. Instead he comes back to them as their fishing guide and breakfast chef—their feeder, in other words—who makes himself known to them by making sure they have plenty of fish and bread to eat. Afterward, he goes out of his way to remind Peter, the disciples' impulsive leader, that following him means they are to be feeders too.

> When they had finished breakfast, Jesus said to Simon Peter, "Simon son of John, do you love me more than these?" He said to him, "Yes, Lord; you know that I love you." Jesus said to him, "Feed my lambs." A second time he said to him, "Simon son of John, do you love me?" He said to him, "Yes, Lord; you know that I love you." Jesus said to him, "Tend my sheep." He said to him the third time, "Simon son of John, do you love me?" Peter felt hurt because he said to him the third time, "Do you love me?" And he said to him, "Lord, you know everything; you know that I love you." Jesus said to him, "Feed my sheep." (vv. 15–17)

In Jesus' day, you could tell how much people earned by the kind of bread they ate. Rich people ate bread made from fine-milled wheat flour. Poor people ate coarse barley cakes, or maybe a handful of parched grain they had to pretend was bread. These days most of us get ours from the grocery store: tortillas, pita, bagels, and naan in the bakery section; heavy 12-grain and thin-sliced white on the bread aisle; Ezekiel bread and frozen biscuits in the freezer case; cornbread and bread-machine mixes on aisle five.

In Jesus' day, no such luck. You made what you could with what you could afford. If you had land, that was the best luck of all. You could grow your own grain and sell the extra to someone else. If you had no land, you had to depend on people who did. You paid what they charged or you did without. In those days, "give us this day our daily bread" was not a sentiment printed on a flour-sack calendar in the kitchen. It was a prayer you prayed for your children's lives. You prayed to be fed so you could feed them too.

In those days, "give us this day our daily bread" was not a sentiment printed on a flour-sack calendar in the kitchen. It was a prayer you prayed for your children's lives. You prayed to be fed so you could feed them too.

Maybe that is why so many of Jesus' teachings involved bread. Follow those teachings through the Gospels and it is hard to believe he was only interested in the health of people's eternal souls. Follow the bread and it is hard *not* to believe that he was just as dedicated to the health of people's God-made bodies on earth.

Have you ever counted the bread stories in the Gospels? There are dozens of them, even after you take out the parallel stories that show up in one or more Gospels, such as the feeding of the five thousand, the feeding of the four thousand, and the Last

Supper. Tucked in between all of these, there is also a famous no-bread story.

"'Take no bread'" (Mark 6:8 NCV), Jesus told his disciples when he sent them out two by two to minister in his name—an odd teaching, on the face of it. Shouldn't he have blessed some bread and tucked it in their backpacks in case they or anyone else needed it—a super loaf that just kept multiplying in the backpack and never ran out?

But Jesus did not do that. Instead, he told his disciples to take no bread. Maybe he did not want them to start thinking of themselves as the "haves," going to bestow their bounty on the "have nots." Maybe he wanted to make sure they had to rely on the kindness of strangers instead of supplying their own needs. When they came into a new town—breadless—they would either find someone with a hospitable heart or they would go to bed hungry. What better training could he have devised for future feeders than to remind them that when God answered their prayer for daily bread, God did it through other people?

"'Blessed are you who are hungry now,'" he said in the Sermon on the Plain. The word is "happy" in some translations—"'happy are you who are hungry now.'" That's another odd teaching in any culture that views having plenty to eat as a happier state of affairs than having none. But Jesus could tell just by looking that a lot of the people following him around were scraping by on less than their fair share of food.

Some of them did not know where their next bread was coming from, and their whole bodies told him they had soaked up the shame of thinking this was somehow their fault—that being hungry meant there was something wrong with them, that they were less blessed, less beloved of God than people who had more to eat. So Jesus fixed that first, before he ever offered them any bread. "'Blessed are you who are hungry now,'" he told them with such authority that their shoulders straightened right up.

Yet this was not the same as telling them that their lot in life was to stay hungry. "'Blessed are you who are hungry now, for you will be filled,'" he said. "'Blessed are you who weep now, for you will laugh'" (Luke 6:21). Jesus saw something more than hunger in their futures, in other words. He saw them being filled and counted on his disciples to get busy with that right away.

"'Give to everyone who begs from you,'" he told those who came to him for instruction, "'and do not refuse anyone who wants to borrow from you'" (Matt. 5:42). The Sermon on the Mount is full of this sort of thing. "'Is there anyone among you who, if your child asks for bread, will give a stone? Or if the child asks for a fish, will give a snake?'" (7:9–10).

Add to those teachings the stories that happened around supper tables—at Levi the tax collector's house, where Jesus was criticized for the low-class company he kept; at Simon the Pharisee's house, where a woman bathed his feet with her tears; in the large upper room where he ate his last Passover meal with his friends, reminding them that it was better to serve than to be served. Add those stories to the list, and the trail of bread crumbs starts to look more like a lighted path.

In Jesus' day, bread was so central to people's lives that there was no way to talk about politics, economics, class, or religion without eventually getting around to who had enough bread and who did not. That meant it was not possible to talk about bread very long without talking about the justice of systems that awarded some people with plenty of bread and left others with none. What created the chasm between the rich man who feasted sumptuously every day and the poor man Lazarus who lay at his gate? One of them had too much bread; the other had none. What separated the sheep from the goats? One group gave food to the hungry; the other gave none.

One of the most famous bread stories in the Bible involves Jesus turning a few loaves of bread into enough to feed thousands of people, but why did he do that? His disciples wanted him to send the people away, perhaps remembering how he had sent them off with no bread in their bags either. Following the same logic, wouldn't it have been better for the crowd to break up and go stimulate some hospitality in neighboring villages the same way they had?

Apparently Jesus was too worried that the people in the crowd would never make it, that they were already so blessed with hunger that they might not have the strength to go very far. "'I have compassion for the crowd,'" he said, "'because they have been with me now for three days and have nothing to eat; and I do not want to send them away hungry, for they might faint on the way'" (Matt. 15:32). Here is a teacher who does not separate body from soul. He wants his followers to have more than words to eat. So he decides to make them some food right where they are.

If you are paying attention, there might be something scratching at the door of your subconscious right about now. Isn't there another story about bread in the Gospels—one that took place in another wilderness—when the devil tempted Jesus to make bread out of stones so no one ever had to go hungry again? Jesus said "no" that time. "'One does not live by bread alone,'" he said that time, "'but by every word that comes from the mouth of God'" (Matt. 4:4). So why has Jesus changed his mind? Why does he decide to make food in one wilderness but not the other one?

Here is something that is easy to miss: Jesus *never* turns stones to bread—not in the wilderness, not on the beach, not anywhere. He never makes manna rain from heaven. He never creates food ex nihilo. He always works with what his disciples give him. When he asks his disciples to feed the crowd and they give him exact numbers so he will understand how little they have (two fish and five loaves), he ignores their math along with their insecurity and asks them to bring him what they have.

Then he makes more of it (they add; he multiplies) without ever cutting his disciples out of the equation. His miracles depend on their willingness to give him what they have, because he "takes no bread" either. He carries no bottomless backpack full of Super Bread so that he can be the one-man solution to a world of need. Instead, he relies on his followers to remember what he taught them when he sent them out two by two: when God answers the prayer for daily bread, God does it through other people.

The same thing happens near the end of John's Gospel—with fish and bread again, but on the beach this time—*after* Jesus' resurrection, when you would think that for once he might give his followers something for nothing—but no. "'Bring some of the fish that you have just caught'" (John 21:10), Jesus says to his old friends, though they can see the charcoal fire behind him already laid with fish on it, and bread. Why can't they just eat that?

They cannot just eat that because it would not be Communion without some of their fish too. They cannot eat it because they cannot be his disciples without becoming feeders too. So Simon Peter brings Jesus some fish, Jesus adds it to the feast, and when everything is ready they watch him do what they have seen him do so many times before. He takes the bread and gives it to them. Then he does the same thing with the fish.

It is how they know it is the Lord—because he feeds them body and soul—not like spiritual babies who cannot bring anything to the feast (though there are times when they feel like that) but like grown-up partners in his feeding ministry, followers of the word made bread whom he commissions to go on feeding the flock.

> Do you love me? *You know I do.* Feed my lambs.
> Do you love me? *You know I do.* Tend my sheep.
> Do you love me? *You know everything; you know I do.* Feed my sheep.

I guess we could have a long discussion about who those sheep are, exactly. Do only Christians need apply? If you have ever been fed, body and soul, at a supper table where you broke bread with friends (or friendly strangers), then you know the answer. This is a story for anyone blessed with hunger.

When you break bread, the bread opens up. When the bread opens up, so does the table. When the table opens up, so does your heart. When your heart opens up, so do your hands—reaching out for some of what you have to hand it to someone else—only to discover that you have more instead of less. This is how the miracle goes on happening, again and again. You follow the bread, and the bread leads you to life—not only for you, and not only for your flock, but for every lamb of God.

Piedmont College Chapel,
Athens, Georgia
February 19, 2011

Chapter Twenty-Two

Practicing Resurrection

Mark 16:1–8

*When the sabbath was over, Mary Magdalene, and Mary the
mother of James, and Salome bought spices, so that they might go
and anoint him. And very early on the first day of the week, when
the sun had risen, they went to the tomb. They had been saying to
one another, "Who will roll away the stone for us from the entrance
to the tomb?" When they looked up, they saw that the stone, which
was very large, had already been rolled back.*

—Mark 16:1–4

Happy Resurrection Day! May the news of Christ's risenness
touch the dead spots in your heart and bring them back to
life, so that you become part of the good news that flows forth
from this place today. May you be springs of living water in all
the dry places on this sweet, parched earth. May the fresh life
that God has given you spill over to freshen all the lives that
touch yours—in your homes, in your work, in your schools,
and in your cities. May you be Easter people, this day and
forevermore.

I have probably overthought this sermon. Easter is a tough
day to preach. Why do you think I am here today instead of the
university chaplain? Good Friday is much easier, all in all, since

most people are more familiar with suffering and death than we are with resurrection. Resurrection is so difficult from so many angles that most Christians are content to think of it as something metaphysical that happens after we die. However we do or do not understand it, the basic reasoning is that since God raised Jesus from the dead and took him to heaven, God will do the same thing for those who believe in him.

So far, so good. But if that is the best we can do, then today becomes the day we thank God for what will happen when our lives are over, and Christian faith becomes the faith of those who care less for life than afterlife. I would have called this an exaggeration until I heard one of my Religion 101 students say it in plain English. "I love studying other religions," she said, "because they have so much in them about how to live. This is different from my own religion, Christianity, which is about going to heaven when you die."

When theologian Harvey Cox taught a class called "Jesus and the Moral Life" at Harvard College, he left the resurrection off his syllabus. One reason was because Christian faith was a prerequisite for belief in the resurrection, and not all of his students had it. Another reason, he said, was because the resurrection "stood on the borderline between the historical and the mystical." So Cox ended his course with the crucifixion, spending the last few sessions of the class discussing some of the different takes on the moral significance of Jesus' life that have arisen in the centuries after his death.

The course was hugely popular, growing every year until Cox finally had to move to a theatre usually reserved for rock concerts. His students pressed him on resurrection, however, and not just the Christians. They wanted to know why Cox was leaving out the climax of the story, the part that made Jesus different from Moses, Muhammad, or the Buddha. Listening to them talk, he discovered that the closest parallels some of them had for Jesus' resurrection were the stories of Dracula or the Terminator. So he decided to add the resurrection to his syllabus, but not before he had done his own research.

Chief among his surprises was the discovery that stories of raising the dead in the Hebrew Bible had nothing to do with achieving immortality. They were all about enacting God's justice. "They did not spring up from a yearning for life after death," Cox wrote, "but from the conviction that ultimately a truly just God simply had to vindicate the victims of the callous and the powerful."[1] To restore a dead person to life is to strike a blow at mortality, Cox pointed out, but to restore a *crucified* man to life is to strike a blow at the system that executed him.

To restore a dead person to life is to strike a blow at mortality, Cox pointed out, but to restore a *crucified* man to life is to strike a blow at the system that executed him.

This changes the way today's story reads, at least for those who don't mind God getting mixed up in politics. According to the Bible Jesus grew up with, when God brought a dead person back to life, it meant that God's reign was very near. And if God's reign was very near, then the reign of the callous and the powerful was very over, in truth if not in fact. For anyone who could read the signs, an empty tomb was the signal that God's justice was on the move—not later on in heaven, but right then on earth.

So of course the women were scared when they saw the stone rolled away from the tomb. They had come to conduct a funeral, not a revolution. They had come to grieve, not to organize.

Even if they weren't up on their messianic theology, they knew they had lost more than their beloved friend. They had also lost their best hope for a new kind of life on earth.

When Jesus was alive, it had been possible for them to imagine a world in which poor people were blessed, sick people were healed, and old people did not have to worry about who would care for them once they could no longer care for themselves. When he spoke, it had been possible to imagine a world in which children could lead the way, lepers could retire their bells, and people with nothing to eat in the middle of nowhere could find themselves at a picnic for five thousand, with twelve baskets to spare. It had even been possible to imagine a world with no Romans in it, patrolling the streets in their metal breastplates and pointy helmets, barking their orders, demanding their taxes.

Jesus' vision of peace and justice was so different from theirs. In the world where Caesar was Lord, military might was the key to peace, power legitimized Rome's right to rule other people, and fear was the surest way to keep the populace quiet. There were benefits of course, at least for those who supported the imperial agenda, but the problem with eating at the emperor's table was that you got addicted to the rich food.

So when the Lord Jesus showed up with food of his own— nothing fancy, just some stale loaves and dried fishes—speaking of peace through justice, of love as the alternative to control— well, people noticed. Unlike the other Lord, he was not armed. Unlike the other Lord, he told people *not* to fear. Yet when he spoke, his words rang with such authority that demons fled, faint hearts revived, and even those dead with despair sat up to take another look around.

This was such good news that there was no way to shut up about it. Jesus was the one they had been waiting for. With evidence like that, who could doubt it? When the time was right, he would act—decisively—to set things right again. He would send the Roman conquerors home to beat their swords into plowshares. He would wipe away the tears from all faces. He would destroy the shroud that is cast over all peoples and swallow up death forever.

That was the hope, at least, but when the Lord Caesar's people heard the news, it sounded anything but good to them. Who wanted a plowshare? They had not gotten where they were by putting their trust in farm tools. They put their trust in swords. So they sent some people with swords to arrest the Lord Jesus, who was not armed, and by the next afternoon he was dead. End of news. Story over.

What this means is that when the women came to anoint his body, they were not just coming to mourn their dead friend.

They were coming to mourn their dead hope. They were coming to lay to rest their dead vision of the way things might have been, the future he had helped them imagine. Jesus wasn't the only one who died. They were *all* dead now.

According to Mark, the first clue the women had that the funeral wasn't going to happen was that the tombstone was not where it was supposed to be. They had been worried about who was going to move it for them. Maybe they even hoped that no one would, so they could go back home and say they had tried to get in without actually having to go in.

It was a dangerous place for them to be seen, after all, at the tomb of a folk hero executed by the state. If they had listened harder, they might have heard camera shutters clicking in the bushes, making pictures for the "Wanted" posters that would go up later that afternoon. If the Committee on Un-Roman Activities wanted to wipe out the rest of the nest, all they had to do was follow the women back home. The two Marys and Salome might as well have been wearing T-shirts that said, "This way to the men." But they weren't that scared yet. They weren't *really* scared until they ducked inside the tomb and saw the young man dressed in white sitting there.

"'Do not be alarmed,'" he said, because they were so *clearly* alarmed. "'You are looking for Jesus of Nazareth, who was crucified. He has been raised; he is not here. Look, there is the place they laid him. But go, tell his disciples and Peter that he is going ahead of you to Galilee; there you will see him, just as he told you'" (16:6–7).

Now *that* was news, though not the kind you were likely to read in the *Imperial Times*. Lord Caesar had failed to silence Lord Jesus. The crucified one had been raised. The dead one was not there. He had gone ahead to Galilee—back to where the story began—to begin the buzz all over again.

Please note that the young man in white did not say that Jesus was going ahead of them to heaven. He said that Jesus was going ahead of them to Galilee, which meant that God's hope was alive on earth. His disciples might not recognize him when they saw him. He might not be able to explain what had happened to him, and he would not stay with them forever. But he was waiting for them, which meant that the Romans had failed. Their system of justice was no match for God's justice, which had kicked their death sentence to the curb and breathed new life into the Lord Jesus. That's what the women were supposed to go tell the disciples and Peter: *it's not over yet.*

But they didn't, at least not according to the oldest version of Mark's Gospel. In that version, which we just heard all the way to the last verse, the women "fled from the tomb, for terror and amazement had seized them; and they said nothing to anyone, for they were afraid" (v. 8). In Mark's struggling Greek, the ending is even more abrupt: " . . . and no one anything they told," it reads, "they were scared, you see, for . . ."

For what?! Mark doesn't say, but he thinks you see.

They were scared, you see, for as wrecked as they were by Jesus' death, they knew how to behave in the face of death. You view the body, you seal the tomb, and you go back to the house to eat fried chicken with the neighbors. You accept the finality of what has happened and you get on with your life, diminished as it is. But when the tomb is empty and the body is gone? *They were scared, you see, for* they didn't know how to behave in the face of death's undoing.

They were scared, you see, for even though they had caught Jesus' vision and decided to follow him, they were still stuck with this guilty relief they felt when they realized how many things they didn't have to believe, do, or hope anymore. At least with death you can stop trying so hard. *They were scared, you see, for* they weren't sure they wanted to move mountains again.

They were scared, you see, for if the Lord Jesus was risen from the dead then so were they. Lord Caesar could go on ruling the world the same old way, but now that they knew what limited damage violence could do to God's cause, there was a whole new way opening up ahead of them. *They were scared, you see, for* death had lost its grip on them, and all of a sudden there was nothing to hold them back.

Mark didn't know exactly what we would be scared of all these years later. He just knew we would be. By ending his Gospel right in the middle of a sentence, he also left us free to decide how it ends. What will we make of the resurrection? How will we practice it ourselves?

Because God knows we need practice. Death may be beat, but it hasn't hit the ground yet. Lord Caesar may be gone, but his successors aren't out of business yet. That's why we need this meal of bread and wine we're about to share, to remind us that God's hope is alive on earth. It's not over yet.

Hear the good news, friends. Though wounded, peace lives. Though killed, justice rises. Though buried, love goes ahead of us to Galilee; there we will see him, just as he told us.

Cannon Chapel at Emory University,
Atlanta, Georgia
Easter Sunday 2006

Chapter Twenty-Three

Believing Thomas

John 20:19–31

A week later his disciples were again in the house, and Thomas was with them. Although the doors were shut, Jesus came and stood among them and said, "Peace be with you." Then he said to Thomas, "Put your finger here and see my hands. Reach out your hand and put it in my side. Do not doubt but believe."

—John 20:26–27

There aren't many "Week Later" stories in the Gospels. Mark is in such a hurry at the end of his that he wraps things up with the empty tomb. Matthew adds a few lines about Jesus appearing to the disciples in Galilee, commissioning them to carry on. Luke tells the story of a stranger who met up with two disciples on the road to Emmaus on Easter evening, but the encounter didn't last long. The minute the disciples recognized the stranger as he broke bread with them at supper, he was carried up into heaven and out of their sight.

John is the Gospel writer who lingers on what it's like to be a disciple after Easter.

He's the only one with a famous Week Later story—the one you just heard—about Jesus and a disciple named Thomas. The Bible says his nickname was the Twin, but no one calls him that anymore. Now he's known as Doubting Thomas, because he had some trust issues that the other disciples did not. He was one of the Twelve, just like Peter, James, and John, but he was unlike them too. Thomas was not one of the inner circle, whom Jesus took with him to places where the others did not go. In spite of his nickname, the Twin stood apart from the crowd.

Earlier, when Jesus was bent on going to Lazarus' home in Bethany, deep in enemy territory, everyone else tried to talk him out of it but Thomas said, "'Let us also go, that we may die with him'" (11:16). When Jesus sat down at the Last Supper table and told the disciples not to be afraid, that they knew where he was going, Thomas alone said, "'Lord, we do not know where you are going. How can we know the way?'" Later, when Jesus appeared to his disciples after his death, Thomas alone was missing. "'We have seen the Lord,'" they told him when he came back, but Thomas held out. "'Unless I see the mark of the nails in his hands,'" he said, "'and put my finger in the mark of the nails and my hand in his side, I will not believe'" (v. 25).

These days, after a round of really good therapy, Thomas might identify as a sensing type, who takes information in through his five senses and trusts experience more than words. Jesus' metaphors must have driven him crazy. *I am the bread of life. I am the gate for the sheep. I am the vine; you are the branches.* While all the intuitive-type disciples were saying, "Ohhhh, yes, I see," poor Thomas was probably saying, "Where? I don't see anything. Point! Where is it?"

So he's not acting out of character in this morning's story; he's acting very much in character. While the writer of the Fourth Gospel makes an example of him, it is done for our benefit. The famous story of Doubting Thomas is offered to everyone forever after who will never have the opportunity to put our fingers in the mark of the nails in Jesus' hands, or to put our hands in his side. "Have you believed because you have seen me?" Jesus says to Thomas once he has seen Jesus for himself. "'Blessed are those who have not seen and yet have come to believe'" (v. 29).

Believing is a huge deal in John's Gospel. Mark uses the verb thirteen times in his Gospel; Matthew uses it nine times and Luke, seven. John uses it over *ninety times* in his Gospel.

> "For God so loved the world that he gave his only Son, so
>   that everyone who believes in him may not perish but
>   may have eternal life." (John 3:16)
> "I am the resurrection and the life. Those who believe in me,
>   even though they die, will live." (11:25)
> "Do not let your hearts be troubled. Believe in God, believe
>   also in me." (14:1)

The word is always a verb in John's Gospel. To believe is to trust what God has done in Christ, and to act as if it were true. To believe is to wash one another's feet. To believe is to abide in love. To believe is to lay down one's life for one's friends. In John's Gospel, Jesus is not interested in what we think or feel. Jesus is interested in how we act.

In our own day, I am afraid that believing has lost most of its motion. The word has sat down and become an overweight noun that separates those who are "in" with God from those who are "out." Christian beliefs have replaced Christian believing, so that if you ask someone what it means to believe in Jesus, what you often get is a list of propositions that person has accepted to be true: I believe that Jesus is the Son of God, that he was born of a virgin, that he died for our sins, that he was resurrected from the dead, that he will come again to judge the living and the dead.

If that list sounds familiar to you, then you may have been taught that being certain of these things will save you a world of trouble. All you have to do is accept the truths that have been handed down to you and stop asking questions about divine realities beyond your grasp. All you have to do is believe what you have been told, and you can go to sleep at night with an untroubled heart.

There's nothing deeply wrong with that. It's more or less what John says at the end of today's reading. He says he wrote his Gospel so people would have all the information they needed to believe that Jesus was the Son of God. But here's what's interesting: the story John tells has some powerful doubters in it, and his narrative wouldn't be the same without them.

A week earlier, when Mary Magdalene came home breathless from the graveyard to tell Peter and the Beloved Disciple that the stone had been moved from in front of Jesus' tomb, they didn't take her word for it. Instead, they left her where she stood and went running to see for themselves. The Beloved Disciple got there first, John says, but he didn't go in. Peter went in, examining everything that was left inside: the linen wrappings that had been used to swaddle Jesus' body, the cloth that had been on Jesus' head rolled up in a place by itself. Peter did not know what to make of them, apparently, but when the Beloved Disciple came in behind him and saw the same things, he believed on the spot.

Mary didn't. After the two disciples went away, she stayed right where she was, weeping inconsolably outside Jesus' tomb. When she finally got up the nerve to look inside the tomb, she didn't see fabric; she saw two angels dressed in white sitting a body's width apart, one where Jesus' head had been and one where his feet had been. The angels asked her why she was crying, and she said it was because someone had taken Jesus away and she did not know where they had laid him. That's what Mary believed: that someone had taken him away. Then she turned around and saw Jesus—only he must not have looked like himself, because she didn't know it was him. Or maybe she just couldn't believe what she saw.

John doesn't say, but my point is that there's a lot of seeing without believing in this story, so why does Thomas take all the heat?

Some of you know Elaine Pagel's work on the Gnostic Gospels, which include the Gospel according to Thomas. Her theory is that Thomas and the Beloved Disciple (aka John) were competitors in the early church, with different convictions about the good news that God had embodied in Jesus. According to Thomas, the good news was that Jesus came to illumine the divine light in us all, which each of us is called to seek until we find. According to John, the good news was that Jesus alone was the light of the world, come to grant eternal life to all who believed in him. For reasons we can talk about later, Thomas's Gospel did not make the cut when it came time to choose what would be included in the New Testament, but John's Gospel did—including his portrait of Thomas as the dissident disciple who was the last to believe in Jesus.

But if John meant to portray Thomas in an unflattering light, he did not altogether succeed. I asked a bunch of people this week just to make sure, and most of them said they knew they were supposed to disapprove of Thomas but they didn't. They liked his honesty. They knew where he was coming from. He was the person in the story who was most like them, and it helped them to think that someone who was *right there* also had trouble believing that Jesus had risen from the dead.

"'Unless I see the mark of the nails in his hands,'" Thomas said, "'and put my finger in the mark of the nails and my hand in his side, I will not believe'" (20:25). If that was a faithless thing to say, Jesus didn't seem to mind. A week later, he made an encore appearance, coming back to the same house, to the same disciples, to say the same thing to Thomas that he had said to everyone else. "'Peace be with you'" (v. 26), he said—or, in the language of the times, "Be whole." Then he gave Thomas exactly what Thomas wanted, which was more than he had given any of the others. Jesus offered himself to be touched.

"'Put your finger here,'" he said to Thomas (v. 27), so close that Thomas could smell his breath. "'Reach out your hand,'" he said to Thomas (v. 27), so close that Thomas would not have had to reach very far. But according to John's Gospel, Thomas never did. The generosity of the offer alone was apparently enough for him. "'My Lord and my God!'" (v. 28) he declared without a doubt, becoming the last of the disciples to believe.

But what did Thomas believe, exactly? I wish I knew. How could you be certain of anything after a week like that? What had been certain before was what anyone could see: dead men stayed dead, bodies stayed in tombs, Caesar was Lord of all the earth, and love was powerless before soldiers with hammers and huge nails. Then Sunday happened, and everything was up for grabs. What the disciples saw that week and the week after was beyond belief, so that's where they went—beyond the safe certainty of belief into the sublime uncertainty of faith.

How could you be certain of anything after a week like that? What had been certain before was what anyone could see: dead men stayed dead, bodies stayed in tombs, Caesar was Lord of all the earth, and love was powerless before soldiers with hammers and huge nails. Then Sunday happened, and everything was up for grabs.

"Those who seek should not stop seeking until they find," Jesus says in the Gospel of Thomas. "When they find, they will be disturbed. When they are disturbed, they will marvel, and will reign over all."[1]

"'Have you believed because you have seen me?'" Jesus says in the Gospel of John. "'Blessed are those who have not seen and yet have come to believe'" (v. 29).

He was talking about us, you know. He was talking *to* us, with some kind of crazy confidence that what happened with Thomas could happen again and again, turning doubt to faith and trouble to astonishment in this Week After and all the weeks after to come.

Trinity Episcopal Cathedral,
Portland, Oregon
Second Sunday of Easter
April 23, 2006

Chapter Twenty-Four

Lady Lazarus

Acts 9:36–43

Now in Joppa there was a disciple whose name was Tabitha, which in Greek is Dorcas. She was devoted to good works and acts of charity. At that time she became ill and died. When they had washed her, they laid her in a room upstairs. Since Lydda was near Joppa, the disciples, who heard that Peter was there, sent two men to him with the request, "Please come to us without delay."
—Acts 9:36–38

During Easter season, resurrection is high on the list of things that unite Christians. Whatever we make of it, whatever questions we continue to have about it, this up-from-the-grave thing, this love-is-stronger-than-death thing, is central to Christian faith—not just that it happened to Jesus, but that because of him it is in our futures too. "We look for the resurrection of the dead," we say when we say the Creed, "and the life of the world to come."

If nothing else, this affirmation means that we expect our life-giving community with God and one another in *this* world to continue in the *next*. We trust that there is no expiration date on it—that it is durable, not disposable—and that the God who made us once can make us again, in any world of God's own choosing.

No one can prove resurrection, or disprove it either. I don't even know anyone who can explain it very well. So why go on affirming something that cannot be proven or explained? Maybe it is wishful thinking—although most of us can think of people we do *not* wish to be reunited with in the world to come.

I still remember a widow I visited soon after her husband died. That he died before she did was a great surprise to everyone who knew them both. She was very ill—had been for years—and she relied on him for everything from toast in the morning to turning out the lights at night. He reminded her of that pretty often, too. Caregiving did not come as naturally to him as playing golf. Then one day she heard a big crash in the bathroom and he was gone just like that. People from the church poured in to see her, pulling chairs up to her bed and saying all the usual things:

"Well, at least you know right where he is."

"He went ahead of you to get things ready."

"You'll be together again soon."

On the day I am remembering, she looked up at me with big pleading eyes and said, "Will I *never* get away from him? This world *and* the next?"

Now I let other people do most of the talking about "the life of the world to come," because we imagine it so differently, and no one knows for sure. Even Jesus was a little vague on the subject after he returned from the dead. All we really have are a handful of crossing-over stories, and the very great freedom to decide—both individually and together—what we will make of them.

Today's story from the book of Acts may be the most ignored resurrection story in Scripture. Everyone knows about Lazarus, but what about Lady Lazarus? Tabitha, I mean—or Dorcas, depending on whether you speak Aramaic or Greek—raised from the dead by the apostle Peter and restored to the community of widows in Lydda who could not imagine life without her.

Technically it is a resuscitation story, since Tabitha is restored to life in this world and not the life of the world to come, but that does not explain why it gets such small press. Is it because the story is in Acts and not in one of the Gospels? Is it because Peter did the raising and not Jesus? Is it because Tabitha was a she and not a he?

She was a disciple, Luke says—using the feminine form of the word that shows up only here in the New Testament. Her name meant "Gazelle." She was devoted to good works and acts of charity. Yet none of this protected her from falling ill and dying, in case we needed reminding. The best people die the same way the worst do—the only difference being that the best may have some friends so reluctant to let them go that they send for the most powerful help they can think of—Peter, in this case, who had just healed a paralyzed man in nearby Joppa.

"Please come to us without delay," two of Gazelle's friends begged him, so Peter got up and went with them. It was eleven miles from Joppa to Lydda, so there was that much delay at least, but it is hard to know what the hurry was about. Tabitha was dead. Her friends had already washed her body and laid it out.

When Peter arrived to see for himself, Luke says, the same two disciples who had fetched him from Joppa led him upstairs into a room full of weeping widows. No one said a word to him. They just cried and held out their arms so he could see the clothes Tabitha had made for them while she was still alive.

I do not know how a man was supposed to appreciate something like that. Maybe the widows thought he would notice that Tabitha had made all the tunics out of the same bolt of cloth. Or maybe they thought Peter could tell just by looking that the clothes were too good for them, made from fine stuff they could never have afforded on their own.

Whatever it was, Peter was less interested in the clothes than he was in the disciple who had made them. The first thing he did was put all of the crying women outside, which meant there were no witnesses in the room. Then he knelt down to pray, though we do not know what he prayed. When he was ready, Luke says, Peter turned to "the body"—not "Tabitha," but "the body"—and said, "'Tabitha, get up'" (v. 40) (as in "'Lazarus, come out'").

And Lady Lazarus did. She opened her eyes, she saw Peter, and she sat up. Then Peter offered her his hand and helped her rise, as if he had just talked her out of buying a pair of shoes that were too tight for her. Once the saints and widows saw she was alive,

Luke says, word spread throughout Joppa, and many believed in the Lord.

It sounds like a perfectly good story to me, but according to one of my academic sources it is not. There are several details missing from the story that really ought to be there, this source points out, just as there are several details *present* in the story that really ought *not* to be there. The problem is not who is in the story or where it occurs. The problem, according to this scholar, is that the story lacks *theological clarity*. He's a terrific scholar, by the way. He got me thinking about things I would never have noticed if he hadn't pointed them out.

For instance, why did Peter fail to invoke the name of Jesus when he told Tabitha to get up? He did it when he healed the paralyzed man in Joppa. "'Jesus Christ heals you,'" he said to the man, "'get up and make your bed!'" (9:34). Why didn't he say the same thing to Tabitha? And why did he send everyone out of Tabitha's room before he healed her? Isn't the whole point of a miracle to have as many witnesses as possible?

Then there is the problem of Tabitha's good deeds. Isn't it a mistake to point out that she was devoted to good works and acts of charity? There was nothing like that in the Lazarus story, or the story of the paralyzed man either. The only thing those two had going for them was that they needed help—that they were *beyond all human help*—not that they were great helpers themselves. So why mention the good works, the acts of charity, the tunics and other clothing? Do you want people to think Tabitha *sewed* her way to new life?

These are the kinds of things my source pointed out. Since the text offers no interpretation of these anomalies, he said, there is a limit to its helpfulness. An odd miracle may make an impression, but what kind of impression? People may come to believe because of it, but what do they believe? To avoid misunderstanding, he says, "the miracle needs to be clothed in explicit theological meaning."[1]

What an odd statement. We are excused from paying too much attention to a story in the Bible because it does not line up theologically? As far as I can tell, that is less of a problem for most people than the fact that they are not able to reproduce this miracle no matter where they line up theologically. They too pray for people they love who are dying if not dead. They too call on the most powerful help they can think of, but their prayers do not work the same way Peter's did. Their Gazelle's eyes stay closed. Her too-tight shoes stay on her feet, while they stain their tunics with their tears.

I have a friend who reports miraculous things to me from time to time. No resurrections yet, unless you count the spiritual kind, but he tells me about other things that defy the usual laws of nature: lights that appear in the dark, people who get well without doctors, turtles that say significant things to him. I try to listen as best I can, but last time I got irritated.

"So *what*?" I said. "I'm sure that's wonderful for you, but if it doesn't happen to everybody then why does it matter? What is it supposed to *mean*?" (I was using different words from the biblical scholar, but I heard the echo: "the miracle needs to be clothed in explicit theological meaning.")

My friend said, "It means you don't know how things work. You think you know, but you don't."

"Huh," I said.

"Like when Jesus came back from the dead," he said. "People thought they knew how things worked, then they found out they didn't. That's an important thing to know."

He had a point. How does a fig tree set its buds while there is still snow on the ground? How does a setting hen turn an egg into a chick? How does a fax machine turn print into electrical pulses? I know these things work, but I don't know how—so why can't there be other things at work between this world and the next that I don't understand?

One of my favorite saints is Nicholas of Cusa, a fifteenth-century German cleric who wrote a book called *On Learned Ignorance*. There are at least three kinds of ignorance that show up in those who seek God, he says.

First there are those who *do not know* that they do not know. They think they know everything they need to know about God.

Then there are those who know that they do not know but who think they *ought to know*. They know that they don't know everything about God, but they're still trying to remedy that.

Finally, there are those who *know that they do not know* and who receive this learned ignorance as God's own gift. It relieves them from the terrible burden of thinking they have to know everything God knows. It frees them to live in a state of perpetual wonder. It saves them from ruling out new life for themselves and those they love on the grounds that they *know how things work* and life like that isn't possible.

This is very high-level ignorance, Nicholas says. Those who accept it do not know where the wind comes from or where it goes, but they can live with that because they trust God *does*.

I think Gazelle's friends were that kind of people. They wouldn't have sent for Peter in the first place if they hadn't already let go of what they thought they knew about life and death. Jesus had messed up their certainty about that. Peter too. When he brought their friend back to life, it reinforced their ignorance in the best possible way. *Praise God! We don't know how things work!*

We are the people who don't know how things work but who trust that God does, whose high-level ignorance frees us to live in unusual ways and say unusual things.

But even if Peter had come out of Tabitha's room and said, "I'm so sorry; she's gone," I think that same ignorance might have saved them in the end. *We don't know how things work. But God does, so let's go do what we know how to do: let's get Peter some food, say our prayers, and tell stories about Tabitha all night long while we wait to see who God will raise up in this community next.*

Isn't that how it works? We are the people who don't know how things work but who trust that God does, whose high-level ignorance frees us to live in unusual ways and say unusual things, even things as odd as, "We look for the resurrection of the dead and the life of the world to come."

What will that look like? How does it work? Who will be there and who will not? Hear the good news: *we do not know*—and we can live with that, because we trust God does.

First Presbyterian Church,
Durham, North Carolina
Fourth Sunday of Easter
April 25, 2010

Chapter Twenty-Five

The Bright Cloud of Unknowing

Matthew 17:1–9

Six days later, Jesus took with him Peter and James and his brother John and led them up a high mountain, by themselves. And he was transfigured before them, and his face shone like the sun, and his clothes became dazzling white. Suddenly there appeared to them Moses and Elijah, talking with him.

—Matthew 17:1–3

The story that we have just heard defies interpretation, although that has not stopped legions of interpreters from trying. It is the luminous story of a mystical encounter, not only between God and God's Beloved but also between those at the center of the cloud and those who watch. Those at the center are Jesus, Moses, and Elijah. Those who watch are Peter, James, and John. And then, of course, there are all of us watching all of them, most of us laboring under the illusion that our job is to figure out what the story *means.*

I am not sure where we got this idea, but it seems to dominate the way many of us read the Bible. Give us a passage of Scripture and we will put on our thinking caps, doing our best to decipher the symbols, read between the lines, and come up with the encoded message that Jesus or Luke or God has hidden in the passage for us to find. The idea seems to be that the story itself is chiefly a suitcase for conveying the meaning inside of it. Discern the content of the story and you do not have to go rummaging around inside of it every time it comes up. Instead, you can pull the meaning out of it and place it neatly folded in a file where you can find it the next time you need it.

Give us a passage of Scripture and we will put on our thinking caps, doing our best to decipher the symbols, read between the lines, and come up with the encoded message that Jesus or Luke or God has hidden in the passage for us to find. The idea seems to be that the story itself is chiefly a suitcase for conveying the meaning inside of it.

In the present case, the most common decoded message is that Moses stands for the law, Elijah stands for the prophets, and Jesus, of course, is the Messiah. By singling Jesus out as "'my Son, the Beloved'" (v. 5), God sets the gospel over the law and the prophets. Listen to *him*, says the voice from the cloud. There are usually two auxiliary meanings as well—one about how it is better to keep your mouth shut in the presence of the holy than to blurt things out like Peter does, and another about how the purpose of such mountaintop experiences is to strengthen us for the climb back down into the valley of the shadow of death, where our real work remains to be done.

For all I know, those are exactly the meanings that Jesus or Luke or God meant for us to get from the story, but I do feel compelled to point out that the passage itself does not say any of those things. Instead, it describes something so beyond ordinary human experience that most of us are perfectly content to watch it from *at least* this far away.

It starts with a long climb up a windy mountain in the fading light of day, hunting for a strong place to pray. No talking for once. No wall of words between you and the others. Just breathing for once, just hearing them breathe, until you cannot tell whether you are breathing or being breathed. Are you hyperventilating?

Sit down. You are here to pray, so get on with it. Pray until you are weighed down with sleep. Pray until it is dark enough to see light through your eyelids where light should not be. You don't *really* want to open your eyes to see where the light is coming from. But you kind of do. But you don't. Then you look.

And there he is: someone you thought you knew really well, standing there pulsing with light, leaking light everywhere. Face like a flame. Clothes dazzling white. Then, as if that weren't enough, two other people are there with him, all of them standing in that same bright light. Who are they? Can't be. Moses. Elijah. Dead men come back to life. God's own glory, lighting up the night. Now they're leaving. Now Peter's saying something.

Tents, we need tents. He thinks we're on Sinai. Someone tell him we're not on Sinai. Now there's a cloud coming in fast that is way more than weather, a terrifying cloud that is also alive. Cutting Peter off. Covering everything up. Smells like a lightning strike. Can't see a thing.

Then a voice from the cloud lifts the hairs on the back of your neck. Fear so fast and primitive, you're bristling like a dog. What's it saying? Not "listen to *me*" but "'listen to *him*'" (v. 5). The Son, the Beloved. Listen to *what*? He's not saying anything. He's shining. Or at least he was. Now he's not. Now it's over. Now what?

If anything even remotely that weird has ever happened to you, then you know why Peter, James, and John were relieved when Jesus told them to keep what had happened to themselves. Supernatural light. Famous people come back from the dead. God talking to you from inside a cloud. Things like that may happen in the Bible, but try talking about them now and someone's going to give you the name of a good psychiatrist. If you have to say anything at all, then you're better off sticking with Bible commentaries. Just say the thing about Jesus surpassing the law and the prophets, poke a little fun at Peter, and bury the rest. It might have been God. Then again, it might have been last night's Thai food.

Most of us are allowed at least one direct experience of God (within bounds)—something that knocks us for a loop, blows our circuits, calls all our old certainties into question. Some churches even require you to produce one as proof of your conversion. But even in congregations that welcome signs and wonders on a regular basis, there seems to be a general consensus that life in Christ means trading in your old certainties for new ones.

Once you emerge from the cloud, you are supposed to be surer than ever what you believe. You are supposed to know who's who, what's what, where you are going in your life and why. You are supposed to have answers to all the important questions, and when you read the Bible you are supposed to know what it *means*. You have your Christian decoder ring, now use it!

But what if the point is not to decode the cloud but to enter into it? What if the whole Bible is less a book of certainties than it is a book of encounters, in which a staggeringly long parade of people run into God, each other, *life*—and are never the same again? I mean, what *don't* people run into in the Bible? Not just terrifying clouds and hair-raising voices but also crazy relatives, persistent infertility, armed enemies, and deep depression, along with lifesaving strangers, miraculous children, food in the wilderness, and knee-wobbling love.

Whether such biblical encounters register in human consciousness as "good" or "bad," they have a way of breaking biblical people open, of rearranging what they think they know for sure so that there is room for more divine movement in their lives. Sometimes the movement involves traveling from one place to another. Sometimes it means changing their angle on what is true and why. Sometimes it involves the almost invisible movement of one heart toward another.

Certainties can become casualties in these encounters, or at least those certainties that involve clinging to static notions of who's who, what's what, where you are going in your life, and why. Those things can shift pretty dramatically inside the cloud of unknowing, where faith has more to do with staying fully present to what is happening right in front of you than with being certain of what it all means. The *meeting* is the thing.

There is no way to be sure, but I think Peter sensed that. When Jesus lit up right in front of him, Peter knew what he was seeing. The Bible calls it God's "glory"—the shining cloud that is the sure sign of God's capital P Presence. When Moses climbed Mount Sinai to fetch the tablets of the law, the whole top of the mountain stayed socked in divine cloud cover for six whole days (Exod. 24:15–18). When Solomon dedicated the Temple in Jerusalem, a dense cloud filled up that huge place so that the priests could not even see what they were supposed to be doing (1 Kgs. 8:11). When Ezekiel had his vision of the four living creatures, he saw them in the middle of "a great cloud with brightness around it and fire flashing forth continually" (1:4).

That's what God's glory looks like, apparently: a big bright cloud—dark and dazzling at the same time—an envelope for the Divine Presence that would blow people away if they looked upon it directly. So God in God's mercy placed a cloud buffer around it, which both protected the people and made it difficult for them to see inside.

Before the cloud rolled in, Peter knew that he was seeing God's glory. What he did not see was a tent of meeting, like the one where Moses met with God during the wilderness years. So Peter offered to set one up—one for each of the great ones who appeared in glory before him. "'Lord . . . if you wish, I will make three dwellings here, one for you, one for Moses, and one for Elijah'" (Matt. 17:4). Peter may not have known what he was saying, but his instincts were good. He knew that he was in the presence of The Presence. He knew that God was right there, and that tent or no tent, he was standing as close as he was ever going to get to the only kind of meeting that really matters.

For those of you who keep the Christian calendar along with the one that says today is March 2, today is the swing Sunday between the seasons of Epiphany and Lent—the day those who follow Jesus look down at our maps and say, "Uh-oh," because it is time to turn away from the twinkling stars of Christmas toward the deep wilderness of Lent. As gloomy as that may sound, it is very good news. Most of us are so distracted by our gadgets, so busy with our work, so addicted to our pleasures, and so resistant to our depths that a nice long spell in the wilderness is just what we need.

No one can make you go, after all. But if you've been looking for some excuse to head to your own mountaintop and pray, this is it. If you've been looking for some way to trade in your old certainties for new movement in your life, look no further. This is your chance to enter the cloud of unknowing and listen for whatever it is that God has to say to you. Tent or no tent, this is your chance to encounter God's contagious glory, so that a little of that shining rubs off on you.

Today you have heard a story you can take with you when you go. It tells you that no one has to go up the mountain alone. It tells you that sometimes things get scary before they get holy. Above all, it tells you that there is someone standing in the center of the cloud with you, shining so brightly that you may never be able to wrap your mind around him, but who is worth listening to all the same—because he is God's Beloved, and you are his, and whatever comes next, you are up to it.

Broadcast on *Day 1*
Transfiguration Sunday
March 2, 2014

Chapter Twenty-Six

Every Singing Creature

Revelation 5:11–14

*Then I heard every creature in heaven and on earth and under the
earth and in the sea, and all that is in them, singing,
   "To the one seated on the throne and to the Lamb
   be blessing and honor and glory and might forever and ever!"
And the four living creatures said, "Amen!" And the elders fell
   down and worshiped.*
                                        —Revelation 5:13–14

Today is a great day to doubt the wisdom of separating "the sacred"
from "the secular," as if they were two realities instead of one. Since
you're in church, today is the third Sunday of Easter. Before the week
is out, you may also become aware that it is the Sunday before Earth
Day. On both counts, the timing is brilliant. What better month
than April to celebrate life—the fact of it, the resurrection of it, the
return of it, the richness of it—not just for us but for every living
creature, plenty of whom sing their loudest hymns this time of year?

The first best thing about April in Georgia is that you can sleep
with your windows open. The second best thing is that you may
not need an alarm clock, because right before dawn somebody
outside starts singing. That wakes somebody else up, who also
starts singing. Pretty soon they are all warming up on their own

instruments, making a symphonic sound that is different every morning.

According to the book of Revelation, that is just the bird section of the singing that will take place on that great-getting-up morning when "every creature in heaven and on earth and under the earth and in the sea, and all that is in them" will crowd around the one seated on the throne and the Lamb to sing "blessing and honor and glory and might forever and ever!"

To get the sound right, then, you have to hold those soprano bird voices in your head while you add the bass voices of lions, whales, and hippopotami to the mix. Then layer in the baritone cows, the raccoon and crocodile tenors. Are those coyotes or alley cats singing countertenor? You decide, but don't forget to bring in the altos: gray dolphins, red foxes, yellow Labrador retrievers.

I don't have a clue what kinds of sounds moles, voles, or earthworms make, but according to Revelation they're in the choir too—"every creature in heaven and on earth and *under the earth* and in the sea, and all that is in them."

This raises an important question: Is a weeping willow a creature? How about a mountain, or a river? I guess it depends on your definition. If a creature is anything made by God, the sky is the limit. Stars, oceans, willows, lava rocks: they're all in the choir. They all get to sing, the same way the hills sing in the Psalms, while the trees of the field clap their hands.

However mute such creatures may seem to us, the Bible says they are all capable of singing. They are just waiting to find their voices. They are just waiting for the good news: that the one seated on the throne has come to free the songs that have been in them all along.

I have been teaching Introduction to the Bible to college students this semester, which has reminded me that most of us see what we expect to see in Scripture (and do not see what we do not expect to see, even when it is right in front of us).

When I show students the two creation stories in Genesis, for instance—one in which God makes human beings on the sixth day of creation, after everything else is finished; and one in which God makes human beings first, "when no plant of the field was yet in the earth and no herb of the field had yet sprung up," most of them can't see two different stories, because they are so sure there is only one.

No one ever told them there were two stories. There is nothing in the Bible that says, "Creation Story Number One" and "Creation Story Number Two." How can there be two? I know what my students are thinking. If God had noticed something like that, surely God would have taken one of them out or at least made sure they matched.

To help them see what is right in front of them, I give them a simple worksheet that helps them track the differences for themselves. This upsets some of them and intrigues others, but by the end of the week 99 percent of them are back to their default settings. It is just too hard to remember things that aren't supposed to be there.

A second strategy is to focus on the first, more familiar creation story, showing them that God made cows and human beings on the same day. Most of the students don't like that at all. Human beings are supposed to be the pinnacle of creation, the best things God ever made—so what are we doing sharing a birthday with *cows*? But that's what the Bible says: the sixth day is living creatures day, when God made "the wild animals of the earth of every kind, and the cattle of every kind, and everything that creeps upon the ground of every kind," including both kinds of humans. "In the image of God he created him, male and female he created them."

At this point, religiously educated students usually remind me that God gave dominion to the humans, not the cows—which is why people eat cows but cows don't eat people, and why humans are allowed to do whatever we want with the rest of creation. This is the divine order of things, they say: humans at the top of the pyramid, the rest of creation underneath. No voice, no vote. Not human? Tough luck.

This leads to another thing I have noticed about the human reading of Scripture, namely that we prefer the parts that are about us—people, I mean. Who *cares* about God's relationship with ostriches or sea monsters? Who *cares* if God brings rain on a desert where no one lives? We like the parts that speak to our condition, the ones that promise us things and tell us how to get them. The parts we like best of all are the ones that grant us special privileges, like the dominion thing.

We like the parts that speak to our condition, the ones that promise us things and tell us how to get them. The parts we like best of all are the ones that grant us special privileges, like the dominion thing.

Since dominion comes in many forms, there is no reason to stop with the humans-over-animals arrangement in the book of Genesis. There are plenty of other "special privilege" passages in the Old Testament, and in the New one too.

Here is one from Paul's first letter to the Corinthians: "Women should be silent in the churches" (14:34). Back when I was full-time pastor, a teacher from a local Christian school asked if he could bring a group of students on a field trip to the church. I said sure, I'd be glad to speak with them. We met in the sanctuary, where the teacher asked all of the questions. The young people were perfectly lovely, very quiet and polite. Later I learned that the purpose of the field trip was for them to experience first-hand a church that did not follow the teachings of the Bible.

Here is another dominion passage from one of Peter's letters: "Slaves, accept the authority of your masters with all deference, not only those who are kind and gentle but also those who are harsh" (1 Pet. 2:18). Sometimes, in class, we talk about how Christians make distinctions between historically conditioned teachings in the Bible and teachings that are true for all time. How do Christians decide which are which? Then, if they are game, we discuss why the teaching about obedient slaves is a thing of the past while the teaching about silent women is still in play.

The problem with dominion is that you need minions to make it work. What good is dominion without someone or something to dominate—other creatures, land, women, slaves, people of other faiths? I am not saying *you* would do that, but some people would. Some people would be happy to find a religion that put them on top and kept them there.

I don't think ours will do that, at least not for very long. It might work if a favorite verse or two told the whole story, but a whole faith won't fit in a single verse. The minute you find one that suits your purposes, along comes another one that messes things up.

> "The Lord God took the man and put him in the garden of Eden to till it and keep it" (Gen. 2:15). *Wait. We have to till it and keep it?*
>
> "For dominion belongs to the Lord" (Ps. 22:28). *But I thought you said. . . .*
>
> "'Whoever wants to be first must be last of all and servant of all'" (Mark 9:35). Last *of all?*
>
> "Think of us in this way, as servants of Christ and stewards of God's mysteries. Moreover, it is required of stewards that they be found trustworthy" (1 Cor. 4:1–2). *Okay, got it.*

If I could change one word in the New Testament, the one I would change is "world," because somehow or another that word has come to mean the world of people. When I hear Christians use it, some use it as shorthand for the fallen creation, while others use it as the opposite of the church. The world is something we are in but not of, a doomed way station on our way to somewhere else. If I could change it, I would leave it untranslated, since the Greek word *kosmos* works fine—better than fine, really, since it sets the word free from human bondage. Listen and see what you think:

> "'For God so loved the *kosmos* that he gave his only Son, so that everyone who believes in him may not perish but may have eternal life.'" (John 3:16)
> "'I am the light of the *kosmos.*'" (John 9:5)
> "'You are the light of the *kosmos.*'" (Matt. 5:14)
> "'Go into all the *kosmos* and proclaim the good news to the whole creation.'" (Mark 16:15)

To whales and hippopotami?
To the whole creation.
To mountains and rivers?
To the whole creation.
Even earthworms?
What part of "whole creation" do you not understand?

How much of the world slides off the page when we read the Bible as a book about God and people instead of a book about God and all creation? We have a part to play, no doubt about it. We even have special privileges, though they may not be exactly the ones we were hoping for.

Our part is to light this cosmos the way Jesus lit it. Our part is to be stewards of God's mysteries. Our privilege is to preach good news to all creation, so that no voice is missing from the choir when it comes time to sing to the one seated on the throne and to the Lamb—sing blessing and honor and glory and might forever and ever.

And the four living creatures said, "Amen!"
And the elders fell down and worshiped.
And so do we.

Trinity Presbyterian Church,
Atlanta, Georgia
Third Sunday of Easter
April 18, 2010

Chapter Twenty-Seven

Who Needs Heaven Now?

Matthew 5:1–12

Then Jesus took his disciples up the mountain, and gathering them
  around him, he taught them, saying:
"Blessed are those whose spirits are low, for the kingdom of heaven is theirs.
Blessed are the sad, for they shall be consoled.
Blessed are the timid, for they shall inherit the earth.
Blessed are those who forget to eat because all they can think about is
  doing good, for they shall be filled.
Blessed are the lenient, for they shall receive leniency.
Blessed are the whole-hearted, for they shall see God.
Blessed are the mediators, for they shall be called children of God.
Blessed are those who are always in trouble for treating the right
  people wrong and the wrong people right, for theirs is the
  kingdom of heaven.
Blessed are you when you are tyrannized on my account.
Rejoice! Be glad, for your reward is great in heaven."
                              —Matthew 5:1–12, au. paraphr.

Then Simon Peter said, "Should we be writing this down?"
Andrew said, "Will this be on the quiz?" James said, "Are we
supposed to know this already?" John said, "You didn't make the
other disciples learn this." Philip said, "I don't have a pen." Bar-
tholomew said, "How many points is this worth?" Thaddeus said,

197

"Would you say the third one again?" Matthew said, "I have to go to the bathroom." Judas said, "What does this have to do with real life?" And Jesus wept.[1]

Yesterday was All Saints Day—not a huge day on the church calendar, but a significant one nonetheless. If Halloween is masks-on day, then All Saints is masks-off day, when we stop to remember just how many people are beloved of God: those we suspected and those we did not; those we can name and those we cannot; those who left their marks on this world and those who vanished without a trace—Saint Teresa and Grandma Lucy, Oscar Romero and Uncle Howard, first-century martyrs and second-grade teachers, saints whose graves we tend and those whom we know no more about than the pile of stones all but lost in the woods.

Today we call them saints not because they performed three miracles or lived exemplary lives. We call them saints because they belonged to God, maybe even showed us a little bit of God, the same way some of us are showing a little bit too, right now, whether we mean to or not. Of course all saints are all sinners too—who doesn't have a dim day, far from the glory of God?— but somehow All Sinners Day doesn't have the same ring. Most of us already know that about ourselves, anyway. It's the saint part that's hard to remember: that we belong to God, that we are beloved, even if God alone knows why.

If you decide to agree that you belong, then one of the hardest things about All Saints Day is realizing what a raggedy-ass crowd you have just admitted to being part of. The Beatitudes I just paraphrased are about as close as you can get to membership requirements, and they don't ask for much: spiritual poverty, mournfulness, meekness, mercy-mindedness, single-heartedness, unwillingness to fight, willingness to get beat up. I guess you could romanticize those virtues. Plenty of people do. We print the Beatitudes on everything from kitchen towels to key chains, for heaven's sake, but if you were to take a tour of the places where such blessed people have traditionally been found, you would visit a lot of jails, funeral homes, courthouses, cheap restaurants, and emergency rooms, as well as some nice homes in the suburbs and a palace or two.

It's a mixed crowd we belong to—more mixed than most of our churches show—but at least we don't have to wonder what a blessed life looks like. Jesus laid that out right at the beginning of his most famous sermon, though his description is so far from what some of us had hoped that we would rather discuss the teaching than act on it.

> How many points is this worth?
> Would you say the third one again?
> I have to go to the bathroom.

Jesus didn't invent the literary form. Beatitudes are short, two-part affirmations that sum up common knowledge about the good life. You can find plenty of them in the First Testament, though don't be surprised if some translations use "happy" in place of "blessed." The same Greek word—*makarios*—can mean both of those, as well as "blissful" or "fortunate."

> "Happy are those who find wisdom,
>   and those who get understanding" (Prov. 3:13).
> "Happy are those whose way is blameless,
>   who walk in the law of the LORD" (Ps. 119.1).

These sayings and others like them function as signposts to a life worth living, but the Bible doesn't have exclusive rights to them. Tune your ears to the pattern and you can probably hear some secular beatitudes circulating around you right now, summing up the common wisdom of our times.

"Blessed are those who go in for regular dental checkups, for they shall keep their teeth." Your dental hygienist didn't say it exactly like that, but you got the message. That's a benign example, but I can think of others. "Blessed are those with sharp tongues, for they shall disarm their foes." That one should be on the home page for Twitter. "Blessed are those with plenty of money, for they shall never know sorrow." That one's a lie, but some people live by it all the same.

I made all of those up, but you can do it too. Just listen to what you are hearing about the good life—from politicians, from advertisers, from famous athletes and best-selling authors—and you can usually hear a beatitude in there somewhere, some truth claim about what will make you happy—or blessed—if you will just accept the view of reality they offer. That's what makes Jesus' Beatitudes so odd. His truth claims don't confirm common wisdom; they actually go against it. "Blessed are the poor in spirit," the sad, the tyrannized.

What does this have to do with real life?

I once worked with a copyeditor who was not a big church-goer. This turned out to be very helpful since she reminded me how churchy my language had become. Beside the word "dea-con," she wrote, "Please define." Beside the word "sacrament," she wrote, "Can you explain?" When I said I didn't know anyone but Jesus who praised spiritual poverty she wrote, "If this is true, is there another way to phrase it? This sounds so negative."

Yes, it does.

In this life, most of us pedal pretty hard to avoid going in the direction of Jesus' Beatitudes. We read books that promise to *enrich* our spirits. We find all kinds of ways to *sedate* our mournful-ness. If there were an audiobook called *How to Become More Meek*, who would write the reviews? With the exception of my copyedi-tor, everyone I know is so used to hearing the Beatitudes by now that it's hard to imagine their original shock value. If only there were one that said, "Blessed are you who suffer from late-stage cancer, for you shall be made whole," or "Blessed are you whose prayers go unanswered, for you shall see God face-to-face."

Like everyone else, I want the second half of the sentence but not the first. I want the comfort, the mercy, the intimacy with God; I want to be an inheritor of the earth and the divine king-dom as well. But if the only way to get to the second half of the sentence is to go through the first, then who in their right mind wants to go?

It helps to remember that the Beatitudes are not moral instruc-tions. The rest of Jesus' Sermon on the Mount will have lots of instructions in it, but not yet. Right here at the beginning, Jesus is not telling anyone what to do. He is telling us how things really are. In one peculiar blessing after another, he connects present human realities with future divine realities in some very unsettling ways. He tells us how things work and then lets us decide whether we want to work with them or not. If we decide we don't, there's really no sense listening to the rest of his sermon, because everything that follows is going to be based on the tipsy worldview of the Beatitudes. Love your enemies, do good to those who hate you. Bless those who curse you, pray for those who abuse you. *Those* are the instructions.

But where has that gotten us, exactly? What *does* this have to do with real life? It has been two thousand years, and the poor in spirit are still with us. Those who hunger for justice are still hungry. The mournful are still blowing their noses, and the excluded are still waiting at the border. The Beatitudes may work for people who can wait until they die for their reward, but meanwhile there are other people who have lost faith in Jesus' promises. They aren't feeling the joy. They need heaven now.

It helps to remember that the Beatitudes are not moral instructions. The rest of Jesus' Sermon on the Mount will have lots of instructions in it, but not yet. Right here at the beginning, Jesus is not telling anyone what to do. He is telling us how things really are.

Since the book of Revelation reveals a different Jesus from the Jesus of the Gospels, I have never spent much time with it. Martin Luther once said that if you weren't crazy *before* you read Revelation, you would be crazy *after* you read it. But if you decide to search out all the beatitudes in the Bible, you'll find quite a few in that last, crazy book of the New Testament.

"'Blessed are the dead who from now on die in the Lord'"
  (14:13).
"'Blessed is the one who stays awake and is clothed'" (16:15).
"'Blessed are those who are invited to the marriage supper of
  the Lamb'" (19:9).
"'Blessed is the one who keeps the words of the prophecy of
  this book'" (22:7).

I have never seen a single one of those on a kitchen towel or key chain. Have you? Maybe that's because Jesus didn't say them all, or maybe it's because there aren't any rewards attached to them. By the time they were written, people had been waiting for Jesus to come back for sixty years or more. Jerusalem had been decimated not once but twice; the Romans were landing hard on Christians and Jews. Past promises were not enough to live on anymore. People needed to be reminded of what to look for when God's real life broke into their real lives in the present—not to evacuate them to heaven, but to bring heaven to earth. The revelatory beatitudes were meant to restore their vision, by reminding them that they were still beloved of God, just as they were.

When you listen to the Beatitudes in the Gospels alongside the beatitudes in Revelation, the ones in the Gospels begin to sound different. You start to notice that the first words out of Jesus' mouth are not "Blessed shall be" but "Blessed are." "Blessed are the poor in spirit"—not because of something that will happen to them later but because of what their poverty opens up in them right now. "Blessed are those who hunger and thirst for righteousness"—not because God is going to fill them up later but because their appetites are so fine-tuned right now. The second half of the sentences still matter—the future promises still hold— but the blessings in the first half are not deferred. Heaven begins now, for any saints willing to sign up.

When people who can't stop crying hear Jesus call them blessed right in the basement of their grief, they realize this isn't something they are supposed to get over soon. This is what it looks like to have a blessed and broken heart.

When people who can't stand up for themselves hear Jesus call them blessed instead of defective, they learn this is not a flaw they need to fix. Jesus sees something in their yielding that is worth blessing right now.

When people who are getting beat up for doing the right thing hear Jesus call them blessed while the blows are still coming, they are freed to feel the pain in a different way. The bruises won't hurt any less, but the new meaning in them can make them easier to bear. Who knows? They may even change the hearts of those landing the blows, while they bring the black-and-blue into communion with each other like almost nothing else can.

This is what the Beatitudes have to do with real life. They describe a view of reality in which the least likely candidates are revealed to be extremely fortunate in the divine economy of things, not only later but right now. They are Jesus' truth claims for all time, the basis of everything that follows, which everyone who hears them is free to accept, reject, or neglect. Whatever you believe about him, believe this about you: the things that seem to be going most wrong for you may in fact be the things that are going most right. This doesn't mean you shouldn't try to fix them. It just means they may need blessing as much as they need fixing, since the blessing is already right there.

If you can breathe into it—well, that's when heaven comes to earth, because earth is where heaven starts, for all who are willing to live into it right now.

Chalmers United Church,*
Kingston, Ontario
Sunday after All Saints Day
November 2, 2008

*A later version of this sermon was given at the Episcopal Church of the Mediator in Meridian, Mississippi, in 2010.

Chapter Twenty-Eight

The Oddest Miracle

John 2:1–11

On the third day there was a wedding in Cana of Galilee, and the mother of Jesus was there. Jesus and his disciples had also been invited to the wedding. When the wine gave out, the mother of Jesus said to him, "They have no wine." And Jesus said to her, "Woman, what concern is that to you and to me? My hour has not yet come." His mother said to the servants, "Do whatever he tells you."

—John 2:1–4

Those of you who have taken even a short course in the Gospels know that the fourth one is an odd duck. In the first three, Jesus doesn't want to talk about who he is (*tell no one*); in the Fourth Gospel, he can't stop talking about it (*did I not tell you?*). In the first three, he teaches in parables (*there was a man who had two sons*); in the fourth one, he gives long speeches (*I still have many things to say to you*). In the first three, he passes around bread and wine on the night before he dies (*do this in remembrance of me*); in the fourth one, he washes feet (*you also ought to wash one another's feet*).

This may not be a different Jesus, but the Fourth Gospel offers a different view of Jesus. For reasons no one can explain, John tells stories about Jesus that Matthew, Mark, and Luke seem never to have heard, including this morning's story about Jesus' first miracle at a wedding in Cana of Galilee. In the first three Gospels, Jesus begins his public ministry by preaching, teaching, and healing the sick; in this one, he begins by turning more than a hundred gallons of water into wine because his mother wants him to.

Even Jesus knows it's an odd thing to do. He may be used to his mother's feminine communication skills. ("They have no wine," she says, the same way your mother said, "The trash is full" or "We're out of firewood.") He may even be used to deflecting her—first by telling her it's not their business, and second by telling her it's not his time. But when she overrules both of his objections—so Mom-like—not by speaking to her son but to the servants ("Do whatever he tells you"), Jesus caves, doing his mother's will instead of his. He turns water into wine, putting the party back on track, though only Jesus, his mother, and the servants know that something miraculous has happened. If it had happened at Downton Abbey, it would have happened downstairs in the kitchen. Yet this is the first of Jesus' signs, John says—the first indication that the Messiah has come into the world God so loves. The sign of the water-turned-to-wine reveals Jesus' glory, giving his disciples reason to believe in him.

Maybe that's why Christians have a hard time letting this story stay as odd as it is. If it's *that* important, we want it to make sense—to mean something other than it seems to mean—if only so it fits better with our ideas of who Jesus is and what he came to do. He revealed his glory prematurely because his mother wanted him to? That can't be right. There has to be more to it than that. I'm sure you've heard the most popular interpretations, but here are a few of them just in case.

This is a story about how Jesus came to fill the old, empty jars of Jewish ritual with the new wine of the gospel. Why else did John include the detail that they were jars for the Jewish rites of purification?

Well, I can think of several reasons. He might have done it because he wasn't sure his Gentile readers would know what the big jars were doing there if he didn't tell them what they were for. He might also have wanted us to know what a really big wedding it was—so many people washing their hands over the course of a week's festivities that the water had run out along with the wine. But if you need Jesus to replace Judaism with Christianity, this explanation may work for you. If you don't like that one, however, here is another:

This is a story about how Jesus blessed the sacrament of marriage even though he never married himself. If you have ever been to a wedding in an Episcopal church, you heard the priest say it like this: "The bond and covenant of marriage was established by God in creation, and our Lord Jesus Christ adorned this manner of life by his presence and first miracle at a wedding in Cana of Galilee." Maybe so. It seems a bit of a stretch to me. Did Adam and Eve get married? I must have missed that part. But if you need Jesus to be pro-marriage, then this interpretation may help. If not, here's another one:

This is a story in which Jesus reveals himself as the messianic bridegroom. By choosing to work his first miracle at an earthly wedding, he foreshadows the day when he will be the groom at a heavenly one. Once the faithful church meets her faithful Christ at the altar (with his Father as the celebrant), the banquet will go on forever and the wine will never run out. This interpretation is really quite lovely, if you can overlook the fact that Jesus says it's not time to do this yet. The revelation is on his mother's timetable, not his.

The least persuasive interpretation I have heard is that *this is a story about how Jesus likes a good party.* While most of us think of him as an ultra-serious savior who only had time for life-and-death things, this story reveals his full humanity. He enjoyed a lavish celebration as much as the next person and was not above using his powers to keep a good one going. Okay, but it still wasn't his idea. I think he was secretly glad when the wine ran out because all he really wanted to do was go home and read.

This was not the feeding of the five thousand, after all. It wasn't even the healing of the ten lepers. It was the restocking of the bar. It was the refueling of revelers who had already had enough to drink. While most of the other signs Jesus performs in this Gospel have meaningful tag lines to go with them ("I am the bread of life," he said after feeding the multitudes; "I am the light of the world," he said before healing a man born blind), it's hard to think of a good line to go with this one. "I am the wine of the party"? But if you need a Jesus who knows how to have fun, this interpretation is for you.

Whether you are partial to any of these explanations or not, the one thing they have in common is their wish to tame this story—to domesticate the miracle so it will lie down and behave the way a good Christian miracle should behave. Even if it won't obey the laws of science, it should at least obey the laws of piety, by yielding a moral that will hold up in front of a fifth-grade Sunday school class. Shouldn't it?

Then there's the whole problem of miracles. Most of us have prayed for one at some time or another. Some of us are sure we have witnessed one, and we are so changed by what happened that we don't care whether anyone else believes us or not. Yet even those who believe in miracles can be crushed by their capriciousness—that one should happen there but not here, to that person but not to me. Others have solved the problem by deciding there are no such things as miracles, or at least none that require supernatural explanations. Northern lights, healthy babies, DNA, dark matter—all of those are miraculous enough, without requiring the suspension of natural law. As for the rest, the skeptics say, they're tricks, or tall tales, or things with logical explanations that no one has discovered yet.

As far as I know, you can hold any of those positions and still be a Christian. You may have to cross your fingers while people on either side of you are confessing the virgin birth or the physical resurrection, but no one's going to kick you out because you can't go there. Jesus never said the Nicene Creed. In fact, he seemed a little disdainful of people whose faith relied on miracles—even in John's Gospel.

When Jesus came back to Cana after a trip to Judea, John says, a man approached him and asked him to heal his dying son. "'Unless you see signs and wonders,'" Jesus said to the man, "'you will not believe.'" It's not hard to hear the resignation in that, but was it a judgment or a statement of fact? Did Jesus think less of the man for wanting him to work a wonder or did he know that's just how things work? People's minds don't change until something messes with them, a little or a lot. People aren't ready to believe anything new until all the tires go flat on their old rides. Whatever Jesus thought, he healed the boy without ever laying eyes on him. "'Go,'" he told the man. "'Your son will live.'" And it was true. When the man got home, his son was well. John concludes the story by saying, "Now this was the second sign that Jesus did after coming from Judea to Galilee" (4:46–54).

Whatever you think about miracles, the Gospels are full of them, and Christians never seem to tire of trying to count them, discount them, name them, tame them. One of the wisest people I know says that's a complete waste of time. "The only purpose of a miracle," he says, "is to remind you that you don't know how things work." Do you believe in miracles? You still don't know how they work. Do you *not* believe in miracles? Maybe you don't know how things work.

I think it's enough to be agnostic about miracles—literally, to admit that you don't know how they work or why—if only to let them illuminate the distance between certainty and faith. I know plenty of Christians who use certainty and faith like synonyms. They need to be certain of something before they can have faith in it. I'd like to hear what they tell themselves while they're boarding airplanes. Who can be certain that thing will stay in the air the whole way? And yet we board.

Sooner or later, though, most of us discover that certainty can only get us so far. You're certain God exists, but there are times when God seems not to be home. You are certain your prayers are answered except when they're not. Does that mean the answer is "no" or that you haven't tried hard enough? Eventually most of us come to the end of the pavement and have to decide how much further we're willing to walk by faith—that is, by trusting things that can't be proved, which will never work in ways we fully understand.

At that point, agnosticism looks a lot more like faith than most people will admit. You don't know for sure what is going to happen next and you can live with that. You're willing to ask for what you want in prayer, but you don't know for sure how God will respond. You don't know how everything works and you're still willing to get on the plane.

In terms of today's story, this makes what Mary does at least as interesting as what Jesus does. She's the person who is most like us, after all, 100 percent human, with no extraordinary powers save her ability to sway her son—but only up to a point. When she reaches the end of what she can do, she becomes agnostic. Once she has told the servants to do whatever Jesus tells them to do, she doesn't know what will happen next and she's okay with that—not only because she knows her son, but also because she knows where certainty ends and faith begins.

Listen again to their terse, three-line dialogue.

Mary: "'They have no wine.'" This is a woman who is certain of one thing: her son can redeem any situation—even one as commonplace as this—if he wants. She doesn't know how. The first sign in John's Gospel hasn't happened yet, so her belief is not based on anything she has seen Jesus do. Her faith in him is its own kind of virgin birth. There's no reason for it; she just believes he can make a difference if he wants. "'They have no wine,'" she says, calling his attention to the problem in hopes of making it his problem, a strategy that he strongly resists.

Jesus: "'Woman, what concern is that to you and to me? My hour has not yet come.'" So what if the wedding guests have drunk up all the wine? A messiah may be good for many things, but catering is not one of them. No one's life is at stake here. The groom may be embarrassed, but he'll laugh as hard as anyone in years to come when the story is told at his expense. But asking Jesus to conjure more wine? What's next—more snacks, more parking places, more wins for the home team? Even if Jesus were inclined to do it, the timing is all wrong. He's not ready to call attention to himself. He takes instructions from his heavenly father, not his earthly mother. His hour has not yet come.

Mary (ignoring him, to the servants): "'Do whatever he tells you.'" If he decides not to do it, that's his decision, but she sees him differently than he sees himself. She doesn't know what goes on inside his head, about what hour it is or anything else. She's the mother of the man, not the second person of the Trinity, and she will not be rebuffed by a son whose birthdays she has remembered for thirty years.

So she tells the servants to do whatever he says, and then she *leaves* it. She doesn't know what Jesus will do next. If he tells them to do nothing, he tells them to do nothing. If he tells them to do something, he can tell them anything he wants—and *this*, I think, is where Mary's certainty turns to faith. She trusts her son has heard her, and she trusts him to do the right thing. More to the point, she trusts that whatever he does or does not do will be the right thing. And that's that. She doesn't say another word about it. Wine or no wine, she's fine either way.

She trusts her son has heard her, and she trusts him to do the right thing. More to the point, she trusts that whatever he does or does not do will be the right thing. And that's that. She doesn't say another word about it. Wine or no wine, she's fine either way.

In every way that counts, Jesus' decision to make the wine is the oddest part of this odd story. His mother has asked him to do something he clearly does not want to do. The timing isn't right. It's not his business—and he does it anyway. He honors his mother. He saves the bridegroom from embarrassment. He makes more wine, though it goes against his own sense of things and launches his ministry before he is ready.

No wonder so many interpreters have spilled so much ink trying to make sense of this story. The reason they fail—I hope—is because the purpose of a miracle is to remind us that we don't really know how things work. All we know is what those in the kitchen knew: (1) that once you ask Jesus for something, the matter is out of your hands, and (2) when he asks you to do something, you do it—at least if you want a taste of his *very* good wine.

First Presbyterian Church,
Delray Beach, Florida
Second Sunday after the Epiphany
January 18, 2015

Chapter Twenty-Nine

Learning to Fall

John 12:20–26

Now among those who went up to worship at the festival were some Greeks. They came to Philip, who was from Bethsaida in Galilee, and said to him, "Sir, we wish to see Jesus." Philip went and told Andrew; then Andrew and Philip went and told Jesus. Jesus answered them, "The hour has come for the Son of Man to be glorified. Very truly, I tell you, unless a grain of wheat falls into the earth and dies, it remains just a single grain; but if it dies, it bears much fruit. Those who love their life lose it, and those who hate their life in this world will keep it for eternal life. Whoever serves me must follow me, and where I am, there will my servant be also. Whoever serves me, the Father will honor."

—John 12:20–26

Hello, you homiletical revelers, you. Look at you! Out of town and off the clock for the better part of a week, happier than you can say to be sitting where you are instead of standing where I am—not because you don't love preaching, but because you do—though there is not enough time, though there is never enough time, though this week may in fact be the first time in ages that you've been able to focus on *anything* without hearing the sirens of parish ministry. Did you remember to turn off your cell phone?

213

One of my favorite movie scenes is in *Zorba the Greek*, when Basil (Alan Bates) turns to Zorba (Anthony Quinn) and asks him if he has ever been married. "Am I not a man?" Zorba replies. "And is a man not stupid? I'm a man, so I married. Wife, children, house. Everything. The full catastrophe."[1] If you can hear Zorba bang his chest when he says that—so proud of his battered heart, so ready to send it back into the ring when the next bell rings—then perhaps you will forgive me for suggesting that you too have embraced the full catastrophe—God, church, ministry. Everything.

This may not be the worst time to do what you do for a living, but it has to be one of the hardest. Some of you are doing a lot more funerals than baptisms, and if something doesn't change soon you might as well turn the nursery into a storage room. Should you change the music? Hold a revival? Send yourself to the Festival of Homiletics? Even your most reliable givers have less to give than they used to, and you have cut everything you *can* cut from the budget but your own position. Does it really make sense for a congregation that size to have a full-time minister?

Or maybe you serve one of those Main Street churches that is holding steady—still attracting families with young children, still offering the programs that bring newcomers through the doors on a regular basis. The same people who support you support the symphony, the public library, the chamber of commerce. You're lucky to have them, the same way they're lucky to have you—though sometimes you wonder if this equilibrium does not depend on the unspoken agreement that you will not upset anyone. Instead, you will continue to lead a church where the music is excellent, the sermons are uplifting, and all the children are happy.

Like the Greeks in John's Gospel, people come to you because they wish to see Jesus, but plenty of them have a particular Jesus in mind. They want to see the Savior in charge of their survival, who will protect them from danger and shield them from despair. They want to see the Messiah with power to raise the dead, who will help them rise above the things that frighten the life out of them—which they don't want to think about, much less talk about, in church. They want to see the Jesus who can give them a *pass* on the full catastrophe.

What a blow, then, to have to tell them what he said when he heard the Greeks were looking for him—that those who love their lives will lose them, that those who hate their lives in this world will keep them, that the only way for a single grain to bear much fruit is to fall to the earth and die. That *is not* the Jesus they were looking for! Do you want to grow your church or don't you?

One of the hardest things about preaching right now is that it's hard to preach the gospel to people who are scared to death of dying. Most of us have gotten used to the idea at a personal level. Yes, I know I'm going to die one day. When that happens, I trust God to know what to do with me and with everyone else as well. You may have a different way of saying it, but however you say it, we have all had plenty of practice—at funerals, at Communion, every time we say the last line of the creeds. Most Christians can talk about death and resurrection without having an anxiety attack.

But shift the subject from an individual life to the life of a congregation and the gospel can all of a sudden sound, well, a little fatalistic? A little short on vision? Churches aren't supposed to die! Churches are supposed to do whatever it takes to stay alive! Say what you want about people giving up their *own* lives for Christ's sake, but my advice is not to start talking about how a church might lose its life for Christ's sake, or sell all that it owns and give the money to the poor, until you are ready to make a professional move.

You might also go easy on the "grain of wheat" saying, whatever the context, since almost no one is interested in learning how to fall into the earth and die. On the whole, we are all more interested in learning to rise—*over, above, through*—whatever is scaring us, whatever is threatening to bring us down, which may help explain why Jesus had so few real followers while he was alive.

I know we're not supposed to say that, but he didn't. There were a lot of people who enjoyed listening to him. He was a good storyteller. There were a lot of people who wanted something from him. Anything they could get, really. There were also some who just signed up for any workshop that looked interesting: Jesus of Nazareth in February, Honi the Circle Drawer in June. People wanted to see Jesus for all kinds of reasons, but real followers—real lay-down-your-life, fall-to-the-ground-with-him people—there weren't a lot of those. Even some of them, once they saw where following him was going, remembered they had something else to do.

When the Greeks came looking for Jesus at the festival, he knew it was time. The future had arrived. The foreigners had come to take the gospel from Judea and plant it somewhere else in their own language, assuring its survival outside the womb. Jesus could have resisted them. He could have said his time wasn't up yet, his message wasn't ripe yet, but he didn't. He knew how bread is made. "'Unless a grain of wheat falls into the earth and dies, it remains just a single grain; but if it dies, it bears much fruit.'"

According to John, this dying isn't about paying a ransom to the devil or suffering the penalty for sin. It's about knowing the way God works and walking that way with eyes wide open. It's about setting your heart on the welfare of your friends—loving them so much that you spend everything you have to keep them in life, even when that means there's none left over for you. Or almost none. When the time comes, there is still one power left to you—not the power to hang on to your life but the power to open your hands and let it go so the truth is plain to see: this is how God makes living bread.

It is not a message that stands well on its own, especially among Christians who would rather not know where their food comes from. When you're scared to death of dying, you don't want a tour of the packaging plant. *Just give me the bread, please. Just wake me up when it's all over.*

Flying here this morning, I sat beside a man who dozed while we were waiting to take off. We were in coach, so we were wedged in pretty tight. The air in the cabin was warm. The sun was coming through the window. The man had his arm on the armrest when he fell asleep, which meant there was no hope of nudging him back to his side. That was okay. The middle seat is rough. So I shifted toward the window, which was a good thing, since about a second later both of the man's hands shot into the air on either side of him, grabbing for something that wasn't there.

You know what happened. He had that falling dream, the one where the bottom all of a sudden drops out from under you and you wake up like someone has hit you with a hundred volts. It's the most natural thing in the world, to want a handhold at a time like that. You don't even have to think about it. The bottom drops out and so do your hands. It's a completely human response to want someone who can save you from falling, which may be why Christians have always been more attracted to the rising part of the gospel than we are to the falling part.

It's a completely human response to want someone who can save you from falling, which may be why Christians have always been more attracted to the rising part of the gospel than we are to the falling part.

Historically speaking, the Jesus movement picked up steam after *that* part of the news got out. Yes, he had died, but it hadn't lasted long. Yes, he had come back with wounds on his body, but they didn't seem to be hurting much. Once people found out that the dying was only temporary and it was over, they *piled* on. Who wouldn't? Everyone loves a winner.

If you ask me, this is why some of us suffer from imposter syndrome in the pulpit—because while we're working so hard not to upset anyone, we *know* better. We know that the falling part and the rising part can't be picked apart like that.

As painful as it is to visit the hospital day after day, watching the person in the bed get more and more translucent, it is also possible to hear how the conversations in the room change.

Healing things are said that could not be said before. Spacious silences open up that no one could have stood before. When the breath finally stops and the tears start coming, there can be as much gratitude in them as grief. It doesn't always happen that way, and no one would have chosen it, but once you've been part of something like that it's hard to deny that there is salvation in falling.

As frightening as it is to ride an economy that is falling—no, rising; no, falling—listening to people talk about losing their insurance, their homes, their ability to provide for their kids, it is also possible to hear some of them saying that they never realized how much stuff they had—too much stuff, really—until they couldn't afford it anymore. They can't believe how excited the kids got the night they ate the snow peas and tomatoes they grew in clay pots on the stoop of the new apartment. It doesn't always happen that way, and no one would have chosen it, but once you've been part of something like that, it's hard to deny that there is salvation in falling.

As awful as it is to serve a congregation that is dying—just twelve or thirteen left on a Sunday morning, and only one of them under sixty—trying to come up with ways to keep things going until the neighborhood changes again, or the culture, or whatever it is that is eating away at the numbers—it is also possible to hear people talking about what it means to *be* church in ways you have never heard them talk before. When one of them suggests it might be time to have a proper funeral for the church and let the building go so a younger congregation can have it— well, it doesn't always happen that way, and no one would have chosen it, but once you've been part of something like that, it's hard to deny that falling to the ground is not the worst thing that can happen to a grain of wheat.

I used to think that the gospel truth was something you had to impose on reality—some impossible thing you had to believe so you could choose the way of life. Now I think it's more about admitting the truth you already know down deep, even if it scares you to death: that when the time comes, you can live small or you can live large. You can hang on to the grain you have or you can gamble it all for love.

When you wake from the dream of falling to find it's not a dream, you can actually *choose* to open your hands, along with your battered heart, which is how you discover the front edge of the good news: not the life *after* falling, but the life *in* falling—all the life you'd have missed if you had clung to the one you had.

If you can trust that, also trust this: God will know what to do with you next.

The Festival of Homiletics,
Minneapolis, Minnesota
May 16, 2011

Chapter Thirty

The Wise and Foolish Church, Part One

Matthew 25:1–13

"Then the kingdom of heaven will be like this. Ten bridesmaids took their lamps and went to meet the bridegroom. Five of them were foolish, and five were wise. When the foolish took their lamps, they took no oil with them; but the wise took flasks of oil with their lamps."
—Matthew 25:1–4

Matthew is at least partly at fault for my trouble sleeping most nights. Age and stress may also have something to do with it, but as a religious person I cannot ignore Matthew's influence on my nighttime script, the one I run when I am not sleeping. It's usually because I have just woken up from a dream in which I am awfully, irrevocably late for something—an exam, an international flight, the last judgment—something that cannot be rescheduled, at which my absence will be duly noted, and my failure to show up will cost me everything that matters to me—*gone*, just like that—because I overslept, or forgot, or wore the wrong clothes. The door that was once open to me is now closed forever. I don't even bother to knock, because I know how the story ends.

The wise virgins are at the wedding and the foolish ones are locked out.

The wheat is in the barn and the weeds are in the oven.
The sheep have gone to heaven and the goats have gone to
hell.

How is it that no one in these stories knows which one they
are until it is too late? I don't know either, so I just lie there in
the dark, obeying the "keep awake" commands from Matthew's
Gospel.

> "'Keep awake therefore, for you know neither the day nor the
> hour.'" (v. 13)
> "'Keep awake therefore, for you do not know on what day
> your Lord is coming.'" (24:42)
> "'Stay awake and pray that you may not come into the time of
> trial.'" (26:41)

What's easy to forget in the middle of the night is that Matthew's stories are not about individuals. They are about communities of things: bunches of bridesmaids, fields of crops, flocks of animals, nets full of fish. The communities are always mixed, and they go on being mixed without much fanfare until the day someone comes to sort them out. Then the differences between them are revealed, so that some go on to glory while others go to the fire, or stand pounding on doors that will never, ever open to them. The stories are not about single persons. They are about groups of people who do not have forever to choose the way of life.

The church I know best is a mixed group of mixed groups—bridesmaids walking around with baskets of fish on their arms, goats loose in the field eating weeds, bushels of wheat piled too close to burning oil lamps, and sheep following bridesmaids around hoping for a bite of whatever is in their baskets even if it does smell like seaweed.

That's way too much chaos for most of us, which may be why we keep trying to sort the groups ahead of time. You don't need me to tell you how well that is going, but in our own minds, at least, most of us are doing our imperfect best to make sure the whole world gets to the wedding. No one wants to be left behind, and it's not just because the outer darkness is so scary. It's because the party inside sounds like heaven. It's because we know the host, because we love the groom, because we cannot imagine any better place to be.

The question is, do we have what it takes to get there? *As churches*, do we have what we need to keep our lamps lit? Some do and some don't, according to Matthew. Some make it to the party in time and some don't. Some are wise and some are foolish, he says at the beginning of the story, counting on us to stay tuned long enough to learn what sets the two groups apart.

But you don't have to wait long for the answer. *Extra fuel* sets the groups apart, Matthew says. "'When the foolish took their lamps, they took no oil with them; but the wise took flasks of oil with their lamps.'"

Since this is a biblically literate crowd, I'm not going into the differences between a parable and an allegory; or remind you that whatever this story is, it appears only in Matthew; or note how interpretations of the story vary widely depending on whether the reader is hunting for divine grace or good works. I know that you know I know. And you know that I know you know. So let's save that for later and get back to the story. Because as much as I love higher criticism, I love a story more—even one with this many holes in it.

The first one is, *why take extra fuel to a wedding?* Do you make sure you have a full red plastic gas can in your car when you go to a wedding? Do you count on things going wrong, or do you assume—based on the last dozen or so weddings you have been to—that your only problem will be finding a place to park once you get there so you don't have to walk too far in your painful shoes?

Of course it's smart to leave extra time to get there, and maybe even to check the pressure in your spare tire, but the extra fuel seems a little obsessive. Why not pack a cooler of extra food too in case you have to wait six hours for the service to start? Why not take your dog and some dog chow, in case you get held up longer than that?

I guess you could call the extra fuel *faith*, but it seems more like *lack of faith* to me. The wise virgins were not content with having *enough* to get where they were going; they wanted *more* than enough. They made sure they had their own backup packs, while the foolish virgins trusted the bridegroom to be where he said he would be. They believed him when he told them when the ceremony would start. Why in the world did they need backup? *They had faith in him.*

So there's another hole: whose fault was it that the foolish virgins ran out of oil? If the bridegroom had been on time, then all ten of the bridesmaids could have walked through the door together. Those with enough oil would have been just fine and those with extra might even have felt a little foolish, with fuel canisters hanging from their satin sashes. *Bridal survivalists.*

If the bridegroom had just been on time, then those virgins could have checked their extra oil in the coatroom and the other five could have avoided going down in Gospel history as double losers: not just foolish but deadly foolish, barred from the party *of* all time *for* all time, because they never stopped to think the bridegroom might be late.

But he was late—*really* late—so late that all ten bridesmaids fell asleep waiting for him, their lamps left burning beside them so anyone who looked in on them could see who slept with her mouth open and who did not. It was midnight when the good news came at last—"Look! Here is the bridegroom! Come out to meet him"—which was exactly what they all tried to do, trimming their lamps before they stood up to shake out their skirts, totally unaware that the sorting of their mixed group was about to begin.

The trouble started right away. Half of the bridesmaids could not get their lamps to burn right because their fuel was almost gone. Bluish flames hovered low over their wicks, sending up smoke signals that spelled "Help!" Looking over at the wise bridesmaids, all busy tipping the oil from their backup packs into their lamps, the foolish ones did what any good Christian brides-maids would do: they asked their friends for help. Isn't that what you would have done? Or to turn the question around, if you had plenty of oil and saw your friends running flat out of theirs, wouldn't you have offered them some of yours? I mean, the bride-groom was *there*. The wedding was *happening*. How much more oil was anyone going to need before they all walked into the light of the banquet hall?

But that's not how it went down. "We won't have enough if we give you some," the wise bridesmaids said, acting out of scarcity when they could have acted from abundance instead. Where was Walter Brueggemann when they needed him?

"Go buy some of your own," they said, which was when the other bridesmaids really did act a little foolish. Where were they going to find a place that sold lamp oil at midnight? And how did they think they were going to get there in the dark? But off they went, and while they were gone the bridegroom fetched away the five who were left.

Maybe those five were the wise ones simply because they stayed put. Maybe if all ten had just stayed put, we would have the story of the ten wise bridesmaids because *nothing*, not even the fear of being exposed with less than enough—*as* less than enough—could make any of them risk missing the bridegroom when he came.

We will never know, because that is not how the story turned out. As it turned out, the bridegroom came and went without ever saying, "Sorry I'm late." He took the five remaining bridesmaids into the wedding banquet with him, and when the others arrived late and breathless themselves—maybe hoping he would wait for them the same way they had waited for him—he refused to open the door to them. "I don't know you," he said, and that was that: the full-of-holes story of the wise and foolish bridesmaids with the last hole at the end.

"'Keep awake therefore, for you know neither the day nor the hour'" (25:13).

"'Keep awake'"? What is he talking about? Shouldn't he have said, "Have oil"? None of them stayed awake! They all fell asleep, the wise and the foolish together. It wasn't staying awake that made the bridesmaids different from each other. It was having enough oil to last until the bridegroom finally showed up, which no one had any way of knowing ahead of time.

Maybe you *have* to turn this story into an allegory to deal with all the holes in it. Either that, or the holes are there because Jesus wanted us to notice them and ask questions about them—to challenge the divisive moral of the story instead of bowing our heads and closing our eyes to it.

Maybe you *have* to turn this story into an allegory to deal with all the holes in it. Either that, or the holes are there because Jesus wanted us to notice them and ask questions about them—to challenge the divisive moral of the story instead of bowing our heads and closing our eyes to it. Couldn't we at least talk about other ways it might have turned out, if the bridesmaids had stuck together instead of splitting up?

As much as I don't like it, I think it's a true story. I think we really do live in a world that has been waiting since dark-thirty for a wedding—waiting so long that plenty of people have decided the bridegroom was a fiction—or a no-show who changed his mind and headed to Aruba with the diamond. I think those of us who are still waiting for him have a lot of explaining to do, both to ourselves and to anyone else we hope to convince to wait with us.

I think there really is some fuel we have been given that it is our job to protect—not only for ourselves but also for those who come after us, so that they too have what it takes to live lit-up lives. We could probably sit here all night trying to agree about what that fuel is, exactly: the historical faith of the church or the free movement of the Holy Spirit, the Sermon on the Mount or the parable of the Prodigal Son, Jesus' life on earth or his death on the cross, as translated by the editors of the NRSV, the NIV, or the KJV.

What we might not realize is that the waiting itself is a strong witness—even in mixed groups with everything from propane camp lanterns to weak flashlights—and that hanging on to each other when some of us run out of fuel shines a brighter kind of light than anything that comes from a lamp. We can sing in the dark if we have to, so that anyone who is lost or late for the wedding can find us. When they do, either because they saw what was left of our light or because they heard our song, they're not likely to care very much whether we're all wise, all wheat, all good. It will be enough that we're here at all, willing to make room for one more mixed-up person on the way.

Wow. My eyes just got heavy. Did yours? I think I can sleep now, at least as soon as we're through here. Not the sleep of the dead, I hope, nor the sleep of the foolish, but the sleep of those wise enough to stay put and stick together while we wait for the bridegroom to come sort us all out.

Columbia Theological Seminary,
Decatur, Georgia
Emergence Now Conference
January 2010

Chapter Thirty-One

The Wise and Foolish Church, Part Two

Matthew 26:6–13

Now while Jesus was at Bethany in the house of Simon the leper, a woman came to him with an alabaster jar of very costly ointment, and she poured it on his head as he sat at the table. But when the disciples saw it, they were angry and said, "Why this waste? For this ointment could have been sold for a large sum, and the money given to the poor."

—Matthew 26:6–9

At the beginning of this conference, I invited the wise and foolish bridesmaids to come teach us something about the church's responsibility to conserve fuel. By God's grace, we have all been invited to a divine wedding, but we won't be carried there on stretchers. We have a journey to make. We have a bridegroom to meet, and while he is famous for many things, being on time is not one of them.

So we know that having enough oil is important. Having enough light is important, since we want not only to see him when he comes; we also want him to see us. We want him to recognize us—to call us by our names—which will be difficult for him if our lamps have gone out, and impossible if we have gone off somewhere to try to purchase more fuel in the middle of the night because ours ran out.

I am pretty sure you cannot buy eschatological fuel. You proba-
bly can't borrow it either, but the oil of the gospel is hardly scarce.
In Matthew's Gospel, Jesus preaches a whole Sermon on the
Mount about the kind of life that lights up the world (5:1–7:28):

> Curb your anger.
> Cut out the insults.
> Be reconciled to your kin.
> Come to terms with your accusers.
> Keep your hands off what's not yours.
> Stay with your partner.
> Keep your word.
> Stop swearing.
> Turn the other cheek.
> Go the second mile.
> Give to everyone who begs from you.
> Make a loan to anyone who asks you.
> Love your enemies.
> Pray for your persecutors.
> Be perfect, as the one who made you is perfect.
> Give alms quietly.
> Pray modestly.
> Forgive others their trespasses.
> Fast discreetly.
> Don't hoard.
> Stop worshiping wealth.
> Go all-out for the kingdom.
> Do not worry.
> Do not judge.
> Notice the log in your own eye.
> Do not be careless with what is holy.
> Ask for what you need.
> Search for what you want.
> Knock freely on doors.
> Do to others what you would have them do to you.
> Enter the narrow gate.
> Do not fall for false prophets.

Do the will of my father in heaven.
Act on these words of mine.

That is a *lot* of oil, and it is the church's job to conserve it—to make sure this fuel is available from generation to generation—so that people know both where it comes from and how to convert the fuel to light for the world. "'Let your light shine before others,'" the Teacher said, "'so that they may see your good works and give glory to your Father in heaven'" (Matt. 5:16).

This is what I am calling the conservative function of the church.

But there is another story in Matthew's Gospel, just one chapter after the story of the wise and foolish bridesmaids. This one concerns an unnamed woman who comes to Simon the leper's house with a jar of costly ointment that she pours on Jesus' head. She is not a sinner—that is in Luke's Gospel. She is not Mary of Bethany—that is in John's Gospel. In Matthew's Gospel, she is just a wasteful woman, as the disciples are quick to note.

They are angry when they see what she does, Matthew says. They think they have been listening carefully to Jesus—not just to his story about the wise and foolish bridesmaids but also to his teachings about the importance of giving alms, feeding the hungry, and rising above their desire for their own comfort. So when the woman interrupts supper to do something so excessive it is impossible to ignore, they make the kind of speeches they think good disciples should make. They object to the waste. They stand up for the poor. They let Jesus know that if they had been consulted first, they would have made a better decision than *this woman* who has just poured out what might have been saved for more judicious use.

That is when Jesus gives them a new teaching: sometimes oil is meant to be spent, not saved—"wasted," if they insist—though that word reflects an understanding of the divine economy that may now be outdated, for Jesus at least. For him, the time has come to spend, not to save—to open jars that have been protected for ages, to pour out the oil that has been conserved for other purposes. To every oil, there is a season?

Since this is a biblically literate crowd, I am not going into the difference between a parable like the wise and foolish bridesmaids and an account of an event from Jesus' own life like the anointing at Bethany—or the literal and symbolic differences between lamp oil and ointment. You know that I know you know. And I know that you know I know.

Instead, I want to focus on the *verbs* in the two stories, which— as different as they are—are both teaching stories that Matthew thought important enough to write down. One of them stresses how important it is to *conserve* what you need to get you through the night; the other stresses how important it is to *pour out* what might have been saved for all sorts of other good purposes but is needed right now to express something that cannot be expressed any other way, before it is too late.

In the story at hand, the pouring out is done on Jesus' behalf, but once you can whistle the tune you hear it all over the place.

When Elijah came to the widow of Zarephath, he asked her for water, which she willingly went to fetch for him. Then he asked her for a morsel of bread, which was when she let him know that he had just asked for the last thing she had left. "'As the LORD your God lives,'" she said to him, "'I have nothing baked, only a handful of meal in a jar, and a little oil in a jug; I am now gathering a couple of sticks, so that I may go home and prepare it for myself and my son, that we may eat it, and die'" (1 Kgs. 17:12).

She had been a good steward until then, conserving the meal and the oil of life as best she could. Then Elijah came and she knew it was pouring-out time. So she made him a cake with everything she had left, and God took it from there. The jar of meal was not emptied. The jug of oil did not fail, though she had poured it out for the prophet who came to her house (vv. 8–16).

When another widow visited the Temple in Jerusalem near the end of Jesus' life, he watched her put her last two coins into the treasury. They were copper, Mark says. They were worth a penny, and they were all she had left. How she had saved them that long was anyone's guess, but it was pouring-out time and she knew it. So she opened her hand and let the coins fall, with no follow-up story about how she went home to find her broken bank put back together again with coins in it to spare.

Her only miracle was that Jesus saw her do it, calling his disciples over so they could see it too. "'This poor widow,'" he said, "'has put in more than all those who are contributing to the treasury. For all of them have contributed out of their abundance; but she out of her poverty has put in everything she had, all she had to live on'" (Mark 12:43–44).

How did he know those were her last two coins? My mother-in-law said he could have spoken perfect French and won all the gold medals at the Olympics if he had wanted to, but my Christology is not quite that high. I think Jesus knew they were her last two coins because he was about to give everything he had too. He recognized the woman's posture, the look on her face. It took a pourer-out to know a pourer-out. He saw himself in her.

The disciples did not call it "'waste'" that time, so maybe they were teachable after all. Or maybe there just wasn't any time left for discussion, with everything Jesus had tumbling out of his own fast-emptying hand. In Bethany, with the unnamed woman standing over him, he finally made his point clear: there is a time to conserve, and a time to refrain from conserving. There is a time to guard the oil, and a time to pour it out. For those of us who mean to be teachable too, one question worth asking is: what time is it now? What are we supposed to be doing with the oil of the gospel that has been entrusted to us?

Matthew would probably have had one right answer to that. All I know is that conservative bridesmaids and wasteful women are both good disciples in his book—even better than the official male disciples who sometimes make foolish speeches about what should or should not be done with the precious resources entrusted to them by God. You can hardly blame them. I mean, half of their problem is that they are so responsible. They have listened so carefully to Jesus that they are trying to do everything he said all the time. But the other half of their problem is that they are paying more attention to what he said in the past than to what is happening right in front of them.

If they were paying attention to what was happening right in front of them, then at least one of them might notice that guarding the oil of the gospel and pouring it out can happen in the very same gesture—for what is the woman in front of them doing but going all-out for the kingdom? Without worrying what will happen to her, she is taking great care of what is holy by casting her pearl-of-great-price before the only one who can see it for what it is. She is acting on the words of Jesus by enacting the Word right in front of him—and he sees it!

"'Why do you trouble the woman?'" he asks his official disciples. "'She has performed a good service for me.'" That's one translation. "'Good work'" is another, but you know how Protestants feel about good works. "'She has done a beautiful thing to me'" is the loveliest rendition by far, but whichever version you prefer, Jesus' meaning is clear: the woman has done a proper and virtuous thing. She has conserved the oil of the gospel by pouring it out.

"'For you always have the poor with you, but you will not always have me.'" That's a siren of a sentence, coming from someone who championed the poor every chance he got. It's an alarm going off, letting everyone else in the room know what only Jesus and the woman have understood until now: his time is up.

But this is no ordinary anointing, which becomes apparent in the very next thing Jesus says. "'For you always have the poor with you, but you will not always have me.'" That's a siren of a sentence, coming from someone who championed the poor every chance he got. It's an alarm going off, letting everyone else in the room know what only Jesus and the woman have understood until now: his time is up. There's no time left to argue about what could have, should have, might have been done with the ointment. It's time to empty the jar, spend the savings, and do a beautiful thing. "'She has prepared me for burial,'" Jesus says, shutting everyone else right up (vv. 10–12).

The woman never said a word, but Jesus was right: what she did for him is known to this day. Her pouring-out story is told in remembrance of her, as Jesus' pouring-out story is told in remembrance of him. I like to think that the wise bridesmaids poured out their oil too, once the bridegroom had come. Who needed a lamp after that?

There are so many ways to honor Christ, to serve the gospel, to renew the fuel by pouring it out. Even when we're afraid to surrender the little bit we have left, all it takes is a turn of the wrist to demonstrate our faith that there's more where that came from, and what a beautiful thing it is to trust the divine excess of God's care. For in this way we let our light shine before others, so that they may see our good works and give glory to the one who taught us how.

Columbia Theological Seminary,
Decatur, Georgia
Emergence Now Conference
January 2010

Acknowledgments

Always being a guest involves always having a host, and I have had more than my fair share of memorably generous ones. Some were sextons. Some were senior pastors. Others were assistants in ministry, whether they assisted with sacraments or management. Some have retired, some have moved on, and others are still serving where I saw them last. I am grateful to them all, and I had a wonderful time remembering them each by name so that I could include them here at the end.

Following the chapters of this book in order, they include Terri Eckert and Donovan Drake at Westminster Presbyterian Church (2018); Nicole Abdnour and John DeBevoise at Palma Ceia Presbyterian Church (2018); Julie Johnson and Laura Mendenhall at Columbia Theological Seminary (2007); Oscar Dantzler, Bruce Puckett, and Sam Wells at Duke Chapel (2010); Shelagh Casey Brown and Ian Markham at Virginia Theological Seminary (2018); David Greenhaw at Eden Seminary (2015); Luis León at Saint John's Episcopal Church (2006); Geoffrey Hoare at All Saints' Church (2016); Andrea Dellinger Jones at Millbrook Baptist Church (2011); Carol Wade and Sam Lloyd at Washington National Cathedral (2007); James Atwell at Winchester Cathedral in England, made possible by Christine Smith (2015); Robert Norris at Royal Poinciana Chapel, made possible by John

Randolph (2014); Maureen Rovegno, Tom Becker, and Robert Franklin at Chautauqua (2016); Peter Wallace at *Day 1* (2019); Pam Driesell at Trinity Presbyterian Church (2014); Sid Batts at First Presbyterian Church (2007); Anne Bonnyman at Trinity Episcopal Church (2010); Maureen Rovegno, Tom Becker, and Joan Brown Campbell at Chautauqua (2012); Ray Cleere and Ashley Cook Cleere at Piedmont College (2011); Susan Henry-Crowe at Cannon Chapel (2006); Marianne Wells Borg at Trinity Episcopal Cathedral (2006); Joe Harvard at First Presbyterian Church (2010); Peter Wallace at *Day 1* (2014); David Burns at Trinity Presbyterian Church (2010); Wayne Hilliker at Chalmers United Church (2008); Doug Hood at First Presbyterian Church (2015); David Howell at the Festival of Homiletics (2011); Sarah Erickson and Steve Hayner at Columbia Theological Seminary (2010).

These are the names I remember from the communities I visited, but the names of those who welcomed, fed, listened, and spoke to me while I was there surpass all reckoning. They reminded me why church was worth getting up for, over and over again. They gave me reason to put words to the faith that was in me and to trust the Spirit to give those words life. They ministered to me as they do to their resident ministers, by allowing us to meddle with what they hold most holy and keeping the sacred conversation going. My deepest thanks to them and to the God who gives us reason to rejoice.

Barbara Brown Taylor
Clarkesville, Georgia
Eastertide 2020

Notes

Chapter 2: Errors about Beauty

1. "Telling Stories: A Conference of Faith and Art" took place in April 2018 as a joint venture of Palma Ceia Presbyterian Church in Tampa, Eckerd College in St. Petersburg, NEXT Church, and *Image* journal.
2. Leslie P. Spelman, "Calvin and the Arts," *The Journal of Aesthetics and Art Criticism* 6, no. 3 (1948): 246–52.
3. Michiko Kakutani, "Iris Murdoch Defends Art against Plato," *New York Times on the Web* (May 21, 1991), http://movies2.nytimes.com /books/98/12/20/specials/murdoch-fire.html.
4. Wendell Berry, "How to Be a Poet," *Poetry* (January 2001): 270.
5. Elaine Scarry, *On Beauty and Being Just* (Princeton, NJ: Princeton University Press, 1999), 12.

Chapter 3: The Dominion of Love

1. James M. Gustafson, *A Sense of the Divine: The Natural Environment from a Theocentric Perspective* (Cleveland: Pilgrim Press, 1994), 87.
2. "Mass on the World," https://teilhard.com/2013/08/05/teilhard-de-chardin -quote-of-the-week-august-5-2013-mass-on-the-world.
3. Ian Bradley, *God Is Green: Ecology for Christians* (New York: Image Books, 1992), 104.
4. "Dog Makes Cell Phone Call to Save Owner's Life," http://www.nbcnews .com/id/13439261/ns/health-pet_health/t/dog-makes-cell-phone-call -save-owners-life/#.XSyqvLh7nUQ.
5. Carl Sagan, *The Dragons of Eden: Speculations on the Evolution of Human Intelligence* (New York: Random House, 1977), 13–17.
6. Barbara Brown Taylor, *The Luminous Web: Essays on Science and Religion* (Cambridge, MA: Cowley Publications, 2000), 42–43.

239

Chapter 5: Paralyzed by Polarization

1. Wes Avram, "Stop Resolving Conflict!" *Reflections: A Magazine of Theological and Ethical Reflection from Yale Divinity School* (Spring 2018), https://reflections.yale.edu/article/lets-talk-confronting-our-divisions/stop-resolving-conflict-wes-avram/.

Chapter 6: What's Your News Source?

1. *Striving towards Being: The Letters of Thomas Merton and Czeslaw Milosz*, ed. Robert Faggen (New York: Farrar, Straus and Giroux, 1997), 101–2.
2. *Striving*, 106.
3. Both the Germanwings crash and Milke's release were reported widely on the news for March 24, 2015; information on both can still be found using any search engine.
4. "Charges Dismissed 'in the Interests of Justice' for 42 Seneca Lake Gas Storage Protesters," *We Are Seneca Lake* (March 19, 2015), http://www.wearesenecalake.com/category/media/.
5. Melissa Lang, "Sacramento City Council Approves Urban Farm Ordinance" (March 24, 2015), http://www.sacbee.com/news/local/article16244966.html.
6. Robert Langreth and Oliver Staley, "Cancer Drugs Boom Spurred by FDA Moving at Lightning Speed," *Bloomberg*, http://www.bloomberg.com/news/articles/2015-03-24/faster-fda-spurs-cancer-breakthroughs-as-drug-approvals-surge.
7. The *Tulsa World* newspaper reports local births daily. My totals are for the week of March 22–28, 2015, as reported at www.tulsaworld.com/.

Chapter 7: The End Is (Always) Near

1. Part of a widely repeated prayer by the English Unitarian minister James Martineau (1805–1900), which can be found in whole at the Harvard Square Library, https://www.harvardsquarelibrary.org/poetry-prayers-visual-arts/james-martineau-prayer/.

Chapter 8: Pre-Gaming the Apocalypse

1. David Brooks, "The Epidemic of Worry," *New York Times* (October 25, 2016), https://www.nytimes.com/2016/10/25/opinion/the-epidemic-of-worry.html.
2. Ta-Nehisi Coates, *Between the World and Me* (New York: Spiegel & Grau, 2015), 97.
3. Colby Itkowitz, "Feeling Anxious Ahead of the Debate? Here's How to Cope with 'Election Stress Disorder,'" *The Washington Post* (September 26, 2016), quoting Steven Stosny, https://www.washingtonpost.com/news/inspired-life/wp/2016/09/26/feeling-anxious-ahead-of-the-debate-heres-how-to-cope-with-election-stress-disorder/.

Chapter 10: Sabbath Rest

1. Anne Lamott, *Small Victories: Spotting Improbable Moments of Grace* (New York: Riverhead Books, 2014), 43.
2. One of many paraphrases of Yerushalmi Kiddushin 4:12, which torah.org translates as "R. Chizkiyah said in the name of Rav: You will one day give reckoning for everything your eyes saw which, although permissible, you did not enjoy."
3. Stephen McCutcheon, "Breaking the Tyranny of Time," *Journal for Preachers* (Pentecost 1991).

Chapter 12: The Good Heretic

1. Amy-Jill Levine, *The Misunderstood Jew: The Church and the Scandal of the Jewish Jesus* (San Francisco: HarperSanFrancisco, 2006), 149.

Chapter 14: The Parable of the Fearful Investor

1. All found in William R. Herzog II, *Parables as Subversive Speech: Jesus as Pedagogue of the Oppressed* (Louisville, KY: Westminster/John Knox Press, 1994), 152.
2. "The Island of Solentiname," accessed November 11, 2011, http://www.stanford.edu/group/arts/nicaragua/discovery_eng/history/solentiname.html.
3. "Nicaraguan Revolution," in *Wikipedia*, accessed November 11, 2011.
4. Ernesto Cardenal, *The Gospel in Solentiname*, vol. 4, trans. Donald D. Walsh (Maryknoll, NY: Orbis Books, 1982), 39–40.
5. Estimates vary from 75 to 130 pounds depending on the kind of talent in question.
6. Herzog, *Parables as Subversive Speech*, 150–68.
7. Hal Bernton and Daniel Beekman, "Portland's Dignity Village Cleared Path for Seattle's Housing for Homeless," *The Seattle Times* (December 17, 2015), http://www.seattletimes.com/seattle-news/politics/portlands-dignity-village-cleared-path-for-seattles-housing-for-homeless/.

Chapter 15: The Widow's Might

1. *The New Interpreter's Dictionary of the Bible*, vol. 5 (Nashville: Abingdon Press, 2009), 506.

Chapter 16: Divine Evolution

1. "Judaism: The Written Law—Torah," *Jewish Virtual Library*, https://www.jewishvirtuallibrary.org/the-written-law-torah.

Chapter 17: Mariam the Magnificent

1. Beverly Roberts Gaventa, "'All Generations Will Call Me Blessed': Mary in Biblical and Ecumenical Perspective," in *A Feminist Companion to Mari-*

ology, ed. Amy-Jill Levine with Maria Mayo Robbins (Cleveland: Pilgrim Press, 2005), 121.

2. Gaventa, 122.
3. Gaventa, 122.
4. Gaventa, 122.
5. Gaventa, 124.
6. Louise Egan, "The First Christmas," accessed December 13, 2014, http://www.doubleestudios.com/christmaspageant/.

Chapter 19: The Wake-Up Call

1. "Pat Robertson Says Haiti Paying for 'Pact to the Devil,'" cnn.com, http://www.cnn.com/2010/US/01/13/haiti.pat.robertson/index.html.

Chapter 20: Bathing Deep

1. Tom Driver, *The Magic of Ritual: Our Need for Liberating Rites That Transform Our Lives and Our Communities* (San Francisco: Harper and Row, 1991), 208.

Chapter 22: Practicing Resurrection

1. Harvey Cox, *When Jesus Came to Harvard: Making Moral Choices Today* (Boston: Houghton Mifflin, 2004), 274.

Chapter 23: Believing Thomas

1. Stephen Patterson and Marvin Meyer, "The Scholar's Translation of the Gospel of Thomas" (verse 2), *Early Christian Writings*, http://www.earlychristianwritings.com/text/thomas-scholars.html.

Chapter 24: Lady Lazarus

1. Lewis Mudge, "Theological Perspective" on Acts 9:36–43, in *Feasting on the Word, Year C, Volume 2*, ed. David Bartlett and Barbara Brown Taylor (Louisville, KY: Westminster John Knox Press, 2009), 428.

Chapter 27: Who Needs Heaven Now?

1. I adapted this idea from an anonymous contribution to the January 31, 1993, issue of *Synthesis: A Weekly Resource for Preaching and Worship in the Episcopal Tradition*.

Chapter 29: Learning to Fall

1. *Zorba the Greek*, directed by Michael Cacoyannis (1964; Los Angeles: Twentieth Century Fox; International Classics, 2004), DVD.